# STUDENTS
# MUST RISE

## Youth struggle in South Africa before and beyond Soweto '76

# STUDENTS MUST RISE

## YOUTH STRUGGLE IN SOUTH AFRICA BEFORE AND BEYOND SOWETO '76

**Edited by Anne Heffernan and Noor Nieftagodien**

WITS UNIVERSITY PRESS

Published in South Africa by:
Wits University Press
1 Jan Smuts Avenue
Johannesburg 2001

www.witspress.co.za

First published in South Africa in 2016

Third impression 2017

ISBN 978-1-86814-919-3 (print)

Cover images: Soweto Uprising Collection, Wits Historical Papers Research
Archive (top); © Anne Heffernan (bottom).

Images in Chapter 7: Soweto Uprising Collection, Wits Historical Papers
Research Archive.

Excerpt from 'A poem for Jose Campos Torres' by Gil Scott-Heron
reproduced with permission, Gil Scott-Heron Estate and Canongate.

Project management: Hazel Cuthbertson
Copy editing: Hazel Cuthbertson and Judith Marsden
Proofreading: Judith Marsden
Printed by ABC Press

# ACKNOWLEDGEMENTS

This book is a collaborative project between the authors, the editors, the History Workshop at the University of the Witwatersrand and the Solomon Mahlangu Freedom College (SOMAFCO) Trust. It arose out of a desire to mark the fortieth anniversary of the Soweto Uprising, and to use that moment to engage critically with the long and deep history of student and youth activism in South Africa. These issues are central to the academic and organisational concerns of the project partners.

The History Workshop represents over 30 years of primarily community-driven South African social history. Through community collaboration and academic research, the History Workshop focuses on histories of people and communities largely left out of broader South African history, and ensures that the histories and materials generated through this are accessible to the people whose lives and spaces they are about.

The SOMAFCO Trust is a South African youth development organisation that draws its inspiration from the history of SOMAFCO, a college which was established by the African National Congress (ANC) in Tanzania with the support of the international solidarity movement during the apartheid years. Today the Trust works to foster education and entrepreneurial development among South Africa's youth.

These two organisations partnered with the scholars and activists whose work is represented here to produce a volume that addresses some of the hidden histories of student struggle over the last sixty years, and to open these histories to as wide an audience as possible. It is a book that, we hope, will be a resource for today's students, and for those in generations to come. Education and access are tenets at the core of the work of both the History Workshop and the SOMAFCO Trust, and thanks to financial support from the National Lotteries Commission and the National Heritage Council we aim to make this book accessible to secondary and tertiary students around South Africa.

**Anne Heffernan, April 2016**

# Contents

# TIMELINE

| | |
|---|---|
| 1910 | South Africa becomes a union |
| 1912 | ANC founded |
| 1913 | The Natives Land Act (Act no 27) placed racial restrictions on land ownership by creating black reserves on 7% of the land and giving whites control of the remaining 93% |
| 1916 | Founding of University of Fort Hare, the first university for black students |
| 1948 | National Party comes to power |
| 1950 | Group Areas Act (also 1957 and 1966) |
| 1953 | Bantu Education Act |
| 1955 | Freedom Charter drawn up |
| 1959 | Extension of University Education Act |
| 1960 | Sharpeville Massacre; ANC and PAC banned |
| 1961 | Founding of Umkhonto we Sizwe (MK) and African Students' Association (ASA); South Africa becomes a republic |
| 1963–64 | Rivonia trialists arrested and tried |
| 1968–69 | South African Students' Organisation (SASO) founded and launched |
| 1972 | Abram Tiro expelled from Turfloop |
| 1974 | Abram Tiro killed by a parcel bomb |
| 1976 | Soweto Uprising |
| 1977 | Steve Biko dies in police custody |
| 1982 | Koornhof Bills |
| 1983 | United Democratic Front (UDF) launched |
| 1984–85 | Vaal Triangle Uprising |
| 1986 | Pass Laws repealed |
| 1990 | ANC unbanned; Nelson Mandela freed from prison |
| 1994 | First democratic election in South Africa; ANC comes to power |
| 2015–16 | #RhodesMustFall; #FeesMustFall |

# Map of South Africa

After union in 1910 there were four provinces in South Africa: Cape Province, Natal, Orange Free State, and Transvaal. During the 1970s and 1980s the government granted "independence" to some of the supposedly self-governing Bantustans (also known as "homelands") that formed part of the apartheid-era administrative system of creating separate areas for blacks and whites. After the first democratic election in South Africa in 1994, these areas were reincorporated and nine new provinces were proclaimed: Western Cape, Eastern Cape, Northern Cape, North West, KwaZulu-Natal, Free State, Gauteng, Mpumalanga and Limpopo.

The names of some cities and towns are being changed in an ongoing process of transformation.

# GLOSSARY

**Afrikaans** Language that evolved from Dutch among settlers in southern Africa during the nineteenth century, and the mother tongue of most apartheid era politicians; still one of South Africa's eleven official languages.

**Afrikaans as a medium of instruction** Policy imposed on some urban black schools during the mid-1970s by the Department of Bantu Education, requiring that students be taught many core subjects (Maths, Science, Agriculture) in Afrikaans rather than English or a mother tongue.

**assegai** Traditional southern African spear.

**banning order** Restrictions on movement (often effectively house arrest), political activities and associations imposed on opponents of the apartheid government.

**Bantu** Term used in colonial and apartheid South Africa to describe a black African person; from the Bantu language group.

**Bantu Education Act, 1953** Act of parliament under which black scholars and students were educated separately from white scholars and students.

**Bantustans** Ethnically segregated, ostensibly independent and self-governing political entities that nonetheless were contained within the borders of South Africa (including Transkei, Ciskei, Bophuthatswana, Venda, Lebowa, Gazankulu, KwaZulu, QwaQwa, KaNgwane).

**Black Consciousness (BC)** Philosophy of psychological liberation for black people in South Africa, developed by Steve Biko and other members of the South African Students' Organisation, which drew heavily on Pan-African and anti-colonial theorists like Frantz Fanon. BC takes black not as a strict racial category, but includes all groups that were oppressed under apartheid (blacks, coloureds, and Indians).

**Black Theology** Theological project under the wing of Black Consciousness and radical Christian activists that draws heavily on Liberation Theology from South America.

**Boers** Afrikaans term for farmers; often used collectively (and sometimes pejoratively) for whites.

**bogoši** Chieftainship or traditional leadership (Sepedi).

**born frees** The generation(s) of South Africans born after 1994, the legal end of apartheid.

**bucket system** Waste collection method used in the absence of municipal sewage infrastructure.

**bush colleges** Pejorative term for the ethnically segregated universities and colleges in South Africa's rural ("bush") areas, including Turfloop, Ngoye, Fort Hare, and many agricultural and technical colleges.

**Cillie Commission** Government commission of enquiry appointed to investigate the events of 16 June 1976 (and subsequent related events), led by Justice Petrus Malan Cillie. The commission sat for eight months in 1976 and 1977, and took testimony from more than 500 people.

**coconut** Pejorative, racist slang term for a black person who "acts white".

**coloured** Racial category in South Africa that describes someone from historically mixed races; includes descendants of indigenous Khoisan peoples and eighteenth-century Asian slaves.

**Congress movement** Refers to organisations that affiliated to or associated themselves with the principles in the Freedom Charter; also indicated affiliation with the banned African National Congress (ANC) during the 1980s.

**dashiki** Brightly coloured West African shirt; popularised as part of a Pan-African cultural turn in the 1970s.

**December holidays** Period when schools and universities (and some businesses) shut down during the southern African summer.

**Dingaan's Day or Day of the Vow (or Covenant)** National public holiday on 16 December during the apartheid era commemorating the white Voortrekkers' "victory" over the Zulu army led by King Dingane kaSenzangakhona and significant for Afrikaner nationalism; since 1994 renamed as the Day of Reconciliation.

**dorpie** Small town, from the Afrikaans *dorp* (town).

**Extension of University Education Act, 1959** Law mandating the establishment of ethnically-segregated universities for South Africa's various ethnic groups; marked the effective extension of the Bantu Education Act of 1953 to the university level.

**#FeesMustFall** Student movement begun at the University of the Witwatersrand in October 2015 to protest the rise of university fees, a barrier of access to tertiary education for poor black students.

**Freedom Charter** Document drafted in 1955 by the Congress of the People – a political ecumenical gathering in Kliptown, Johannesburg – that lays out a vision for a non-racial, democratic South Africa (derivatives charterism, charterist).

**FRELIMO** Frente de Libertação de Moçambique; Mozambican liberation organisation and current party in power.

**Group Areas Act, 1950, 1957, 1966** Acts of Parliament that assigned various racial groups to different residential and business sections in urban areas under apartheid; many "non-whites" were forcibly relocated to the "correct" areas.

**homelands** See Bantustans.

**imvubu** Southern African leather whip, also sjambok.

**Indian** Racial category under apartheid for South Africans with ancestry in the Indian sub-continent.

**Inkatha Freedom Party** Political party formed in KwaZulu in 1975 that supports Zulu minority rights.

**kgosi** King or chief (Setswana).

**knobkerrie** Southern African knobbed stick weapon.

**koma** Initiation (Sepedi).

**Koornhof Bills** Attempts to introduce reforms to the apartheid system through a series of laws (bills) in the early 1980s, while still maintaining the racial separation it enshrined.

**kwaito** South African house music that emerged in Johannesburg in the 1990s.

**Liberation Theology** Theology that emerged from Roman Catholic teaching in Latin America in the 1950s; it situates Christian theology around a discourse of liberating the poor and oppressed.

**Matanzima KD** Leader of the independent Transkei (Bantustan), first as prime minister from 1976, and as state president from 1979. He retired in 1986.

**mbaqanga** Style of South African music originating in the early 1960s, with rural Zulu roots.

**motswako** Genre of hip hop music originating in Botswana in the mid-1990s; popular in Botswana and South Africa.

**Ngoye (also Ongoye)** The University of Zululand.

**outsourcing** The cost-saving measure of an institution contracting the hiring of some staff to a cheaper third-party company that competes for the contract; in the case of universities, such companies provide security, cleaning, gardening and catering services on campuses.

**pass/passbook** Internal "passports" controlling the movement of black Africans, especially workers, under apartheid.

**Pondoland** Rural area in the eastern part of the Eastern Cape which was the site of political uprising in the 1950s against the Bantu Authorities Act of 1951; this is typically called the "Pondoland Revolt".

**Rand/Witwatersrand** Area corresponding to the largely underground geological formation holding the world's largest known gold reserves; visible above ground from around Bedfordview to Krugersdorp as a rocky east–west running ridge; Johannesburg and Soweto are situated on the Rand, as are a number of secondary towns and townships.

**Republic Day** Public holiday on 31 May celebrating

the day South Africa ceased being a British colony and became a republic in 1961. Celebrated until 1994, it was often a source of conflict.

**Rhodes** Rhodes University in Grahamstown, Eastern Cape, named after imperialist businessman and politician Cecil John Rhodes.

**#RhodesMustFall** Student movement begun at the University of Cape Town in March 2015, advocating the removal of a statue of Cecil Rhodes on the campus, as well as an increased rate of racial transformation at the university.

**Rivonia trial** Trial beginning in October 1963 in which anti-apartheid leaders, including Nelson Mandela, were convicted and jailed for plotting against the apartheid regime.

**Robben Island** In Table Bay, off Cape Town, the island location of the notorious apartheid-era prison used to incarcerate political prisoners.

**Ruth First** Anti-apartheid activist and member of the banned South African Communist Party and African National Congress; killed by a parcel bomb in Mozambique in 1982.

**Sekhukhuneland** Rural area in the northern Transvaal (now Limpopo Province) which was the site of political uprisings in 1958 and again in 1986.

**Separate Development** Apartheid government policy that racial groups should be legally forced to be separate and develop (equitably) into their own homogenous societies.

**Sharpeville Massacre** Black protestors burned their passbooks in the southern Transvaal town of Sharpeville on 21 March 1960, led by organisers from the Pan Africanist Congress. The police opened fire on the crowd and 69 protesters were killed.

**Soweto Uprising** On 16 June 1976 secondary school students marched through the townships of Soweto to protest the imposition of Afrikaans as a medium of teaching. Police fired on and killed some of the students, sparking nationwide protests in schools and campuses over the next year.

**Strydom, JG** National Party member and prime minister of South Africa, 1954–1958.

**the struggle** All political organisation and mobilisation against the apartheid regime.

**the system** Name used by anti-apartheid activists for the National Party government and all its attendant laws and institutions that codified and enforced racial segregation in South Africa.

**township** Urban settlement area restricted to black residents (for example Soweto, Alexandra, Sebokeng, Khayelitsha), generally located in proximity to a town designated "white" where many township residents worked.

**toyi-toyi** Form of protest dance.

**tsotsi** Gangster.

**Turfloop** University (College) of the North, now called University of Limpopo.

**Umkhonto we Sizwe (MK)** Armed wing of the African National Congress, launched in 1961.

**Union Buildings** Official seat of the South African government, in Pretoria.

**United Democratic Front (UDF)** Coalition of hundreds of affiliates (from local civics to national student movements and unions) which protested against apartheid and supported the principles in the Freedom Charter; launched in 1983.

**Unity Movement** The Non-European Unity Movement (NEUM), launched in 1943 and revived, after being inactive for decades, in the late 1980s.

**the Vaal (also Vaal Triangle)** Urban triangle in the southern Transvaal (now Gauteng), formed by the three towns Vereeniging, Vanderbijlpark and Sasolburg and a number of townships; site of a major political uprising in 1984.

**Verwoerd, HF** National Party member and prime minister of South Africa, 1958–1966, considered the primary architect of apartheid.

**yellowbone** Slang term for a light-skinned black person.

# ABBREVIATIONS

| | |
|---|---|
| **AAM** | Anti-Apartheid Movement |
| **AERO** | Applied Education Research Organisation |
| **AFM** | Apostolic Faith Mission |
| **ANC** | African National Congress |
| **ANCYL** | African National Congress Youth League |
| **ANC YSS** | ANC Youth and Students' Section |
| **APLA** | Azanian People's Liberation Army |
| **ASA** | African Students' Association |
| **ASB** | Afrikaanse Studente Bond |
| **ASF** | Anglican Students' Federation |
| **ASM** | African Students' Movement, later became SASM |
| **AZAPO** | Azanian People's Organisation |
| **AZASM** | Azanian Students' Movement |
| **AZASO** | Azanian Students' Organisation |
| **BC** | Black Consciousness |
| **BCP** | Black Community Programmes |
| **BPC** | Black People's Convention |
| **BSM** | Black Students' Movement |
| **COSAS** | Congress of South African Students |
| **COSATU** | Congress of South African Trade Unions |
| **CPUT** | Cape Peninsula University of Technology, Cape Town, various campuses |
| **DBE** | Department of Basic Education |
| **EE** | Equal Education |
| **EELC** | Equal Education Law Centre |
| **EFF** | Economic Freedom Fighters |
| **FEDSEM** | Federal Theological Seminary |
| **FMF** | Fees Must Fall |
| **FUBA** | Federated Union of Black Artists |
| **IUS** | International Union of Students |
| **KEF** | Khayelitsha Education Forum |
| **KZN** | KwaZulu-Natal |
| **LRC** | Legal Resources Centre |
| **MDALI** | Music, Drama, Arts and Literature Institute |
| **MEC** | Member of the Executive Council of a province, answerable to the Premier |
| **MEDUNSA** | Medical University of South Africa, now Sefako Makgatho Health Sciences University, Pretoria |
| **MK** | Umkhonto we Sizwe |
| **MSA** | Muslim Students' Association |
| **MSO** | Mhluzi Students' Organisation |
| **NAHECS** | National Heritage and Cultural Studies Centre, University of Fort Hare |
| **NAYO** | National Youth Organisation |
| **NCFS** | National Catholic Federation of Students |
| **NECC** | National Education Crisis Committee |
| **NGO** | Non-governmental organisation |
| **NMMU** | Nelson Mandela Metropolitan University, Port Elizabeth |
| **NPEP** | National Policy for an Equitable Provision of an Enabling School Physical Teaching and Learning Environment |
| **NSFAS** | National Student Financial Aid Scheme |
| **NUSAS** | National Union of South African Students |
| **NWU** | North West University, with campuses in Potchefstroom, Mahikeng and Vanderbijlpark |

| | | | | |
|---|---|---|---|---|
| **OS** | Open Stellenbosch | | **TUT** | Tshwane University of Technology, with campuses in Pretoria, Soshanguve, Ga-Rankuwa, eMalahleni (Witbank), Mbombela (Nelspruit) and Polokwane (Pietersburg) |
| **PAC** | Pan Africanist Congress | | | |
| **PASMA** | Pan Africanist Student Movement of Azania | | | |
| **PET** | People's Experimental Theatre | | **UCM** | University Christian Movement |
| **PYA** | Progressive Youth Alliance | | **UCT** | University of Cape Town |
| **PYCO** | Phomolong Youth Congress | | **UDF** | United Democratic Front |
| **RMF** | Rhodes Must Fall | | **UFH** | University of Fort Hare, Alice |
| **SAAWU** | South African Allied Workers' Union | | **UFS** | University of the Free State, Bloemfontein |
| **SACC** | South African Council of Churches | | | |
| **SADF** | South African Defence Force | | **UJ** | University of Johannesburg |
| **SADTU** | South African Democratic Teachers' Union | | **UKZN** | University of KwaZulu-Natal, with campuses in Pietermaritzburg and Durban |
| **SAIRR** | South African Institute of Race Relations | | **UNISA** | University of South Africa, Pretoria |
| **SANSCO** | South African National Students' Congress | | **UP** | University of Pretoria |
| | | | **US** | University of Stellenbosch |
| **SAP** | South African Police | | **UWC** | University of the Western Cape, Bellville |
| **SASA** | South African Schools Act of 1996 | | **VALIMO** | Vaal Liberation Movement |
| **SASCO** | South African Students' Congress | | **VASCO** | Vaal Student Congress |
| **SASM** | South African Students' Movement | | **VAYCO** | Vaal Youth Congress |
| **SASO** | South African Students' Organisation | | **VCA** | Vaal Civic Association |
| **SCA** | Student Christian Association | | **WCC** | World Council of Churches |
| **SHAWCO** | Students' Health and Welfare Centres Organisation | | **WCED** | Western Cape Education Department |
| | | | **WHP** | Wits Historical Papers |
| **SOARTA** | Soweto Arts Association | | **Wits** | University of the Witwatersrand, Johannesburg |
| **Soweto** | South Western Townships | | | |
| **SRC** | Students' Representative Council | | **WSCF** | World Student Christian Federation |
| **SSRC** | Soweto Students' Representative Council | | **YCL** | Young Communist League |
| **TAC** | Treatment Action Campaign | | **YWCA** | Young Women's Christian Association |
| **TECON** | Theatre Council of Natal | | **ZASA** | Zeerust African Students' Association |

INTRODUCTION

# NARRATIVES OF THE STUDENT STRUGGLE

## ANNE HEFFERNAN AND NOOR NIEFTAGODIEN

The Soweto Uprising of 1976 was a decisive turning point in the struggle against apartheid. In the morning of June 16 thousands of students marched peacefully through the streets of Soweto to demand the scrapping of Afrikaans as a medium of instruction. By the afternoon those students were fighting "the system" – apartheid – as they confronted the armed forces of the state. In so doing, black students, whose numbers had increased significantly since the early 1970s, were fundamentally changing the country's political landscape. Since that time students have held a special place in the collective imaginary of South African history. The historic occasion in 2016 of the fortieth anniversary of the Soweto Uprising provides an opportunity to engage with this imagining, to contribute to the public debate around the roles that black students play in the politics of their country, and to raise certain questions about the way their history has been framed. June 16 has gained even greater significance due to the #FeesMustFall movement of 2015 that once again brought into sharp relief the power of black students. In fact, the "born frees" have consciously connected their current struggles for free and quality education to the struggles of the 1976 generation.

This volume is a collaboration between the History Workshop (University of the Witwatersrand) and SOMAFCO (Solomon Mahlangu Freedom College) Trust. In the midst of the #FeesMustFall struggles both organisations recognised the need to introduce histories of student movements into the national conversations about the nature of contemporary student protests. The chapters here draw on existing work by leading scholars in the field, many of whom were and are student activists in their own rights. They seek to bring some of the most current academic debates over the role of student mobilisation, ideology, strategy, and tactics to a broad public audience. The scope of time and varied geographic locations addressed in this volume intentionally try to amend a narrative that has placed Soweto 1976 at the centre of discussions on student and youth activism in South Africa and to contextualise that moment with reference to the many forms of activism that have taken place in other locations and institutions over the last sixty years. The narratives offered here range from the political inspiration that young rural children took from their mothers' anti-pass campaigns in the mid-1950s, to an analysis of the current surge of protests on university campuses, which began in 2015 under the banners of #RhodesMustFall and #FeesMustFall.

For many of these stories, particularly those in the first half of the volume, a major catalyst of student organisation was the passage of the Bantu Education Act in 1953, and its implementation over the latter part of that decade. Bantu Education enforced the racial segregation of South Africa's primary and secondary schools by law, and situated responsibility for the educational institutions for black students in the Native Affairs Department. Bantu Education also forced mission-run schools across South Africa to cede control to the government, drastically reducing access to quality education for young African learners. It ushered in a tiered system of education, where both the schools students attended and the content of the curriculum they were taught there were based on race. HF Verwoerd infamously declared that education for Africans had to prepare them to be 'hewers of wood and drawers of water, and fit only for manual work'. In 1959, the Extension of University Education Act expanded this system to institutions of higher education and created an ethnically segregated system of so-called "bush colleges". The prestigious University of Fort Hare, which since 1916 had educated generations of African leaders including Nelson Mandela and Oliver Tambo, was brought under government control and only permitted to accept Xhosa students. Two new universities were built, the University of Zululand at Ngoye in rural Natal (now KwaZulu-Natal) and the University of the North at Turfloop in the northern Transvaal (now Limpopo) to cater for Zulu, Swati and Ndebele, and Sotho-Tswana, Shangaan, and Venda ethnic groups, respectively. In addition, the University of the Western Cape (UWC) was founded at Bellville for coloured students, and the University of Durban-Westville was reclassified for Indian students only. An overarching aim behind the establishment of these "bush colleges" was to produce an educated and compliant elite that would serve the Bantustans and other racial administrations.

However, the students on these campuses rejected the racist ideology of the government and university administrations and from the late 1960s forged a new and radical politics under the banner of Black Consciousness. These institutions, without exception, became sites of student organisation and mobilisation against the very structures that were designed to constrain and direct their educations. They feature prominently in a number of the chapters here, from the early politicisation at Fort Hare in the wake of the Extension of University Education Act and its impact on the formation of the African Students' Association (ASA) in the early 1960s, to chapters on pivotal moments of student protest at Turfloop and UWC in the 1970s, and Ngoye in the 1980s. And, as the two chapters on student movements in the post-democratic period suggest, many of these institutions remain sites of student protest today.

From the early 1970s a new social force began to take shape in townships across the country. The rapid expansion of schools, especially secondary schools, meant that by the mid-1970s there were millions of black students in schools. Beginning with a chapter on the history of the ASA, the volume explores the role of primary and secondary school students in changing the content and scale of political debates that had come before. Over the decade and a half following June 16 1976, school students around the country mobilised themselves in different ways and around varied issues, many of which were locally specific. In chapters on the rural Free State, Mpumalanga, Limpopo, Western Cape, Northwest, and the urban townships of the Vaal Triangle, the authors here interrogate the local specificity of many of these protests, and also link them to national trends.

Several themes arch over and throughout each of these individual historic moments and places, each of which are also addressed in their own chapter: these explore the influences of creative culture, religion, and ideology on student activists. Often these played related and productive roles in shaping the context in which students became politicised. Several authors who reflect on their own activism here address the importance of religion, music, poetry, and a panoply of texts – particularly on Black Consciousness and Pan-Africanism – in their own experiences. The interconnected development of Black Consciousness and Black Theology was of crucial importance in influencing students during the 1970s, from urban townships to rural villages. The artistic cultural production of that time often related to one or both of these: the prominence of "black is beautiful" as a slogan, and famous black musicians and artists modelling this by abandoning hair straighteners and skin bleaches, and by donning African prints and clothes that spoke to a Pan-African identity. These are just a few of the examples that are addressed in these chapters.

A new set of social and economic factors influenced student organisation during the 1980s. The resurgence of non-racial politics propagated by the independent trade unions, township organisations, and the Congress movement, prohibitive rent increases for black families around the country, and the contentious relationship between local government and township residents are just some of the issues that the chapters in the second half of the volume explore. Significantly, student activists of the 1970s went on to become influential actors in other spheres of the anti-apartheid struggles. Many went into exile but the majority remained inside the country to build the mass movements that would lead the struggle against apartheid. Activists joined the emerging independent trade unions and civic organisations. They also established new student organisations, such as the Congress of South African Students (COSAS) and thereafter township-based youth movements. As the township rebellion in the 1980s escalated, the streets eclipsed schools as the primary sites of contestation, as youth engaged in increasingly militant confrontation with the apartheid state and its local representatives.

Identity is another theme that cuts across many of the chapters, as student activists commonly grappled with their own positionality in the communities and country they sought to change. Race was a key factor in this regard, but it was never the sole factor. Class, generation, and gender have been perennial considerations for successive groups of activists. Gendered divides in particular influenced many of the student groups discussed here. Young women involved in student movements faced, and continue to face, challenges born of operating within highly patriarchal spaces. The authors here, half of them women and many of them activists, discuss these and other challenges around creating inclusive and intersectional space in their organisations.

As a whole, the chapters in this volume paint a picture of South African students' political engagement that is broader than more conventional histories of the student struggle have suggested. They draw important connections between movements in the last year, last ten years, last forty years, and last sixty years. These transcend many of the usual boundaries that are imposed on South African history, by relating the early 1960s to the late 1970s, by drawing together the experiences of rural and urban communities, and by exploring the continuities in form and content of protest before and after 1994. The volume is not comprehensive but provides a survey of student and youth politics over an extended period. It endeavours to be both informative and readable in doing so. We hope it will contribute to the public debates about the historic and contemporary contributions of student and youth struggles.

Anne Heffernan is a post-doctoral researcher in the History Workshop at the University of the Witwatersrand with particular interest in the history of political activism among students and youth in South Africa, and the role of educational institutions in anti-apartheid protest. Her research focuses predominantly on Limpopo Province, and she is interested in the ways that ideas move through and across communities, particularly via urban and rural linkages.

Noor Nieftagodien holds the South African Research Chair in Local Histories, Present Realities and is the head of the History Workshop at the University of the Witwatersrand. He has published articles and book chapters on aspects of popular insurgent struggles, public history, youth politics and local history.

CHAPTER 1

# A BRIEF HISTORY OF THE AFRICAN STUDENTS' ASSOCIATION

SIFISO MXOLISI NDLOVU

In 1959 a group of students at the University of Fort Hare (UFH) decided to affiliate to the African National Congress (ANC) in order to strengthen resistance to the Extension of University Education Act which had extended the principles of Bantu Education to university level. They particularly objected to the idea that Fort Hare should be reserved for amaXhosa as an ethnic group, which subverted its history as an institution open to black students from across the continent. Following its banning in 1960, the ANC gave increasing attention to students who it believed would be receptive to political mobilisation. At Fort Hare the ANC faced competition for student support, from the Unity Movement in particular, which had a strong presence on campus.

After the initial meeting at Fort Hare, the idea to form a new student organisation was consolidated in 1960 and 1961, and coalesced around the nationwide strike against the establishment of the Republic of South Africa on 31 May 1961. Thabo Mbeki, then a student at the University of Fort Hare and a member of the ANC Youth League, told a mass rally that African students were breaking with their submissiveness and parochialism and identifying themselves with the mass struggle of the oppressed African people. This marked a shift in student protests from the "bread and butter" issues of food, fees and corporal punishment, and towards a more direct challenge to the apartheid system.

The May 1961 student strikes had a definite effect on the character of emerging student organisations. African students increasingly identified themselves with the daily struggle of the oppressed majority, and university students began to accept their secondary school counterparts as equals in the struggle. Later that year these precedents informed the founding principles of a key new student organisation for black South African students, the African Students' Association (ASA).

## The formation of the African Students' Association

The African Students' Association was officially launched in Durban on 16 December 1961, on the same day as Umkhonto we Sizwe (or MK), the military wing of the ANC. This day was an official public holiday referred to as "Dingaan's Day" or "Day of the Vow" by white South Africans. Through its fighting youth, ASA was committed to the eradication of racist laws perpetuated by the Bantu Education Act of 1953 and the Extension of University Education Act of 1959. One of the pertinent questions that the ANC and the ANC Youth League had to address was: 'Do we need another organisation that could help to mobilise oppressed African students?' The decision was taken that the ANC and its Youth League should establish the ASA.[1] The inaugural conference was opened by Reverend GM Sitiwane, the youth secretary of the Methodist Church, and was attended by students from 38 institutions from various corners of the country. In his opening address Sitiwane noted that the success of Bantu Education depended on the cooperation of those whom it was calculated to destroy. He stressed the need for a formidable united front against Bantu Education which he described as a sinister intellectual genocide. ASA pledged itself to staying true to the aspirations of African students for a system of education free from indoctrination and based on universal standards.[2]

Ernest Galo, a student studying law at the University of Natal (Black Section, Durban), was elected the first president of the ASA. The leadership of this student movement included University of Fort Hare students such as Thabo Mbeki, Sipho Makana and Sindiso Mfeyane who were also members of the ANC Youth League:

> We took a decision to form the African Students' Association because clearly NUSAS [National Union of South African Students] could not represent the views of African students. We could not use NUSAS to mobilise youth and students and be more directly involved with struggle for national liberation in South Africa. Its composition and leadership was predominantly white and liberal in terms of ideology. Therefore we had

to form ASA to cater for the relatively small African student population at universities and as [a] result ASA's membership included students from secondary and high schools. Therefore we had much bigger reach … then once the decision was taken some preparatory work had to be done and as a result I had to travel to different parts of the country, including Bloemfontein, Cape Town, Alice [Fort Hare], Kimberley, Johannesburg and various places to introduce them to the idea we are going to form this ASA.[3]

Ernest Galo died in 1965 at Qacha's Neck in Lesotho whilst on his way into exile because, although ill, with the security police hot on his trail, he could not be admitted to a hospital for treatment. The death of Galo thrust the leadership of ASA into Thabo Mbeki's hands. Some of ASA's aims and objectives were to unite African students, to promote their interests and an understanding of their problems, to create a channel through which African students could express their views in an organised manner, and to encourage an interest in educational and cultural advancement of students. In short, after the banning of the ANC, African students wanted to speak and act as part of a legal student body. Their demand was for national unity and their programme was finding solutions to problems plaguing African students throughout South Africa. The nature of African students' socio-political and community work was determined by their quest for freedom regardless of whether they were based in urban or rural areas of South Africa. To ask students to do anything else would be akin to asking them to abandon the oppressed African masses. ASA led the struggle for national liberation within a sphere where the fundamental social question was defined by national oppression and the denial of all rights, including the right of the majority of the people to acquire education. This was a marked departure from the orthodox position that had been followed by African students up to now – the position of "education for certification". This was no longer enough for African students.[4] Barney Pityana remembers:

Part of the reason of affiliating to the ANC was in order to strengthen the resistance to the Separate Universities Act in particular to the idea

that Fort Hare should be reserved for amaXhosa, if you consider the fact
that up until then it was open to black students regardless of their ethnic
background ... I have always said in the South Africa of those days the
importance of the boarding schools was fundamental because we had
students from different parts of South Africa and when these politically
conscious students go back to their home areas they continue to form
different branches of student movements such as ASA. They become the
contact points.[5]

During the 1960s some student activists were jailed, together with other protesters.
Others were banned and consequently ASA was driven underground. As a precaution
the ANC advised ASA members to go into exile in order to obtain further education
and to continue to play a strategic role in the liberation struggle. Walter Sisulu told
Thabo Mbeki to meet with Duma Nokwe and Govan Mbeki and, according to Thabo
Mbeki, the two 'conveyed the instruction rather than the proposal (of the ANC) that
I should leave the country ... they undertook that Oliver Tambo would discuss my
future with me when I had completed my first year at university in the UK'.[6] Rolihlahla
Mandela requested a send-off meeting with some of the youth before they went into
exile in September 1962. According to Mbeki:

We met him [Mandela] at a secret venue in Mayfair [Johannesburg] where
he conveyed his best wishes to the group and issued his last instruction
before our departure. As part of his final instruction, he made two points
to us. The first was that we were ambassadors of South Africa abroad
and that we needed to behave properly. Secondly, he said that as one of
the first groups of ANC students leaving to study abroad there was an
immense responsibility on us to succeed. He said that when the struggle
for apartheid was over we would be expected to play a leading role in the
process of reconstruction of post-apartheid South Africa.[7]

## The ASA goes into exile

As more and more of its student members went into exile, ASA's priorities became focused: it had to be concerned with the question of national reconstruction, and was also expected to supply militants as members of the liberation movement to play a role in the military struggle adopted by the ANC after its banning in 1960. This demanding task was to be attained in alliance with the working youth who were members of the working class.

Though ASA was a legal student organisation, it was forced to work in conditions of illegality. Much of its leadership was incarcerated or was under banning orders and restricted to a particular area. This also applied to activists operating in other political spheres. Police harassment continued unabated and certain activists were not allowed to hold leadership positions within ASA. Such challenges were experienced by Lawrence Phokanoka ("Peter Tladi") who was a member of both the ANC Youth League and the ASA.

Phokanoka was selected as one of the two delegates who would represent the University of Fort Hare at the official launch of ASA in December 1961 in Durban, but he deliberately avoided going because he was opposed to the suggestion that students go into exile, as propagated by Mandela. 'My suspicions were that if I went to the launch of ASA in Durban, we were going straight to the Soviet Union' immediately after the launch. As a result, 'I ducked going to Durban … I really felt I was going to miss this revolution. I would not complete my [Science] degree.'[8] But the security police were determined to nab him and therefore he eventually did leave the country:

> I left Fort Hare in May 1963 … My contact in ASA was Hintsa Tshume
> and a certain Mike Ngubeni. I wanted to join them to do some work, both
> ASA and ANC work. I did not want to leave the country. But they advised
> me that I cannot stay in the country anymore and that they cannot use
> me because the police were looking for me. They were only using people
> who were not known to the police. And eventually in July 1963 I left the
> country through Botswana. And in the same month, when we reached
> Francistown, we were reading the headlines about the Rivonia arrests.[9]

When Phokanoka arrived in Dar es Salaam [Tanzania], like many others before him, he had to make a choice between joining Umkhonto we Sizwe, or continuing with his education. With guidance from friends such as Chris Hani, another ANC Youth League and ASA comrade whom he knew from his days as a student activist at the University of Fort Hare, Phokanoka chose to join the military wing when he arrived in exile:

> Because I came out on an ASA ticket, I was placed in Mandela House which was reserved for student recruits. Luthuli House was a huge house for MK recruits from home before they were sent all over the world for military training ... At Dar es Salaam we were taken to the immigration offices to arrange for new passports as Tanzanian citizens. I was then taken to Mandela House as a student who was going to continue with his studies because I came on an ASA ticket. On the same day I went over to Luthuli House, I had a meeting with Martin [Chris] Hani, the only person I knew in Dar es Salaam. He came to Mandela House to fetch me with a certain old man from Port Elizabeth called Jeremiah Nxapepe, whose real name seems to be Sam Majola. He came with Hani to try and recruit me to join the military wing of the ANC. In fact I no longer wanted to be a student. Even before I left I wanted to be in the military revolution. Now that I had the opportunity to join MK and return to carry out the revolution, the student thing was just not in my mind anymore.[10]

Those who did not join the military wing of the ANC opted for student life and had to prepare for a demanding life in the political trenches as members of the ANC Youth and Students' Section (ANC YSS).

## The formation of the South African Students' Association (SASA)

Several ASA student activists, including Thabo Mbeki, found themselves in exile in the UK in the mid-1960s. Without prejudicing the work of the ANC Youth and Students' Section internationally, they decided to establish the South African Students' Association (SASA), and to include NUSAS members who were in the

UK. The formation of a fully-fledged ASA branch barely a few months after Mbeki and colleagues arrived in the UK had faced specific challenges. There were very few African students from South Africa based in the UK, and ASA, by pursuing an exclusive agenda, had the potential for working at cross-purposes with the majority of South African students who were already active in the Anti-Apartheid Movement (AAM). The students and youth activists supporting the AAM included African students affiliated to ASA and white students affiliated to NUSAS. Mbeki argued that in the UK the struggle had emerged around the AAM. Therefore a major question was whether organising South African students overseas under one banner in order to lead the fight against apartheid was more or less important than seeking ASA's international recognition, as, for example, a member of the International Union of Students (IUS). According to Mbeki, it was also crucial to take into consideration that before ASA's representatives went into exile, other South African student movements had developed overseas branches, for example, NUSAS in Europe and in America. To be fair to NUSAS as fellow compatriots, ASA could not ask these branches to disband in their favour. This complex situation was compounded by the fact that ASA's role in exile was not well defined. It was incapable of being recognised in Western Europe as a representative student body, except in so far as it would act as the Youth and Students' Section of the ANC. Mbeki was also of the view that a proliferation of South African student organisations in Europe without a defined purpose would not be of any help but would rather increase the amount of tension there was likely to be.[11]

The rivalry between ANC and Pan Africanist Congress (PAC) youth and students in exile was still bubbling in full force. Some of the African members on the SASA committee were very keen to adopt a neutral position concerning the rivalry between the two liberation movements. This was because the rivalry rendered SASA (UK) directionless in terms of the politics of solidarity pursued by South African students. Another major problem was that SASA committee members functioned as individuals. Such an approach to student politics was more pronounced in the UK than in other European countries where ANC-aligned students were the leading political force. This difficulty was compounded by the fact that most of the South African students studying in the UK were white. These students were in many ways more strategically placed than students in other parts of the world. Another challenge faced Mbeki and his colleagues.

Unlike his NUSAS counterparts in the UK, he was unable to establish regular contact with ASA leadership inside South Africa. Such contact would have been beneficial, particularly to African students who qualified for overseas scholarships. Also, it was crucial for Mbeki and other ASA members in the UK such as Mhlambiso to consult with their ASA colleagues in South Africa and provide them with feedback concerning the decisions they were taking about solidarity among exiled students.[12] This included the formation of SASA (UK). Mbeki recalls:

> When I was in exile [in] London [at] that time there was no ANC Youth and Students' Section and therefore we were ASA. It was one organising student body so that our students had a home. There was no decision in terms of international affiliations and because ASA was never banned in South Africa we had to be careful and make sure we did not compromise its legality at home by doing strange things outside ... we formed the South African Students' Association (SASA). This was an ANC decision which was that we need to get hold of the South African student population in the UK and therefore the question as how do we do it? We could not say people must come and join ASA and we could not say our people must go and join NUSAS and so we said let us form SASA and attract everybody. We wanted to have access to South African students who had passports. In the end ASA could not survive once we had established the ANC's Youth and Students' Section ... but when I went to meet colleagues at Pan African Youth Movement I introduced myself as a leader of ASA and this had something to do with communicating a message that we are not an exiled student movement confined to London or the United Kingdom but we were home-based and we represent South African students, not South African students in exile or in London.[13]

## Conclusion

Though challenges for present students are different, it is very important for the present student leadership to take heed of one of ASA's main goals, namely, unity against Bantu Education among students at university and secondary schools. The nature of the challenges facing the students rendered the question of dominance by university students irrelevant. The revolutionary spirit of this student body was inherited by the June 16 1976 student movement. Furthermore, the struggle against racism and ethnicity waged by the students during the 1960s was harmonised with struggles waged by workers and other members of society. As a result, a united front against the formation of the Republic of South Africa in 1961 fast tracked the official launch of ASA. The fact that some of the ASA student leaders and membership became the first generation of leaders after the 1994 democratic dispensation is not lost on us. For example, Thabo Mbeki became the president of South Africa, Manto Tshabalala-Msimang became the minister of Health, Joe Nhlanhla became the minister of Intelligence and Sindiso Mfeyane became South Africa's ambassador to Tanzania. Barney Pityana became the principal of the University of South Africa (UNISA), the biggest university, not only in South Africa, but also on the African continent. What makes the lives of these student leaders interesting is their trajectory into leadership positions in the democratic South Africa as a result of their international experience as student leaders. Most of them spent their exile life in both African and European countries. This surely affected their worldview and understanding of geopolitics during the Cold War. The implication is that the present student leaders in South Africa should cease to be parochial when dealing with issues affecting South African students. They should form a united front with their continental and international counterparts in order to address common problems which afflict students through the world. This is what differentiates them from their predecessors.[14]

## Endnotes

1   See interview with Lawrence Phokanoka ("Peter Tladi") by Siphamandla Zondi, Johannesburg, 1 July 2001, in South African Democracy Education Trust (SADET) (ed.). *The Road to Democracy in South Africa: South Africans telling their stories, Volume 1, 1950–1970.* Johannesburg: Mutloatse Heritage Trust, 2008, Chapter 40.

2   African Students Form New Organisation, *New Age*, 21 December 1961.

3   Interview with Thabo Mbeki by Sifiso Mxolisi Ndlovu, Johannesburg, 15 December 2015, SADET Oral History Project (SOHP). See also interview with Essop Pahad by Sifiso Mxolisi Ndlovu, Johannesburg, 21 February 2006, SOHP.

4   UFH, NAHECS archive, Oliver Tambo Papers (OTP)/053/0594/11, African Students' Association issued by Sipho Mbengwane and Thabo Mbeki as external representatives of ASA, 20 November 1967; African Students have a Mission, *New Age*, 4 January, 1962.

5    Interview with Barney Pityana by Sifiso Mxolisi Ndlovu, Pretoria, 14 January 2016, SOHP.

6    T. Mbeki, Oliver Tambo: A great giant who strode the globe like a colossus, in P. Jordan, *Oliver Tambo Remembered*. Johannesburg: Macmillan, 2007, xv.

7    Interview cited in A. Hadland and J. Rantao, *The Life and Times of Thabo Mbeki*. Rivonia: Zebra Press, 1999, 28.

8    Ibid.

9    Interview with Lawrence Phokanoka by Siphamandla Zondi, Ga-Mankopane, 1 July 2001, SOHP. See also interview with Lawrence Phokanoka ("Peter Tladi") by Siphamandla Zondi, Ga-Mankopane, 1 July 2001, in South African Democracy Education Trust (SADET) (ed.). *The Road to Democracy in South Africa: South Africans telling their stories, Volume 1, 1950–1970*. Johannesburg: Mutloatse Heritage Trust, 2008.

10   Interview with Lawrence Phokanoka by Siphamandla Zondi, Ga-Mankopane, 1 July 2001, SOHP.

11   UFH, NAHECS archive, ANC Morogoro Mission, Box 14, The South African Student Association in the UK.

12   Ibid.

13   Interview with Thabo Mbeki.

14   See SM. Ndlovu, South African Youth and Students in Exile: International solidarity as a weapon for national liberation, 1960 to early 1970s, in South African Democracy Education Trust (SADET) (ed.). *The Road to Democracy in South Africa, Volume 3, part 3*, forthcoming.

Sifiso Mxolisi Ndlovu obtained his PhD in History at the University of the Witwatersrand. He is currently the executive director of the South African Democracy Education Trust and is the editor-in-chief of *The Road to Democracy in South Africa* multi-volume series (UNISA Press, ongoing). He is also a professor of History at the University of South Africa.

# CHAPTER 2

# YOUTH AND STUDENT CULTURE
## Riding resistance and imagining the future

BHEKIZIZWE PETERSON

C ulture is a term that is frequently used but it is also one that is often misunderstood. Unfortunately, the notion of culture is habitually raised when people want to explain their assumed difference from others or when they feel the need to justify the upholding of certain ideas and practices that other people have a problem with. Underlying the use of the term culture is the assumption that culture is a quality that is written into our genes and that we are born with based on the ethnic or racial group that we belong to. Such a view regards culture as fixed, static and not open to change or progress. These are some of the reasons why the mention of culture tends to lead to conflict rather than the affirmation of people's identities or our common humanity.

Culture will be considered in relation to the needs and experiences of young people as well as their participation in social resistance and transformation. It is important, therefore, to spell out the two senses in which the term culture will be used in this discussion. These are "culture" as a way of life, and "culture" as a range of creative and intellectual practices that are broadly called "the arts". As a particular way of life, culture refers to a variety of beliefs, rituals and practices (social, economic, spiritual) that groups or individuals develop over time in specific environments. The beliefs, rituals and practices are developed in response to the spiritual, material, intellectual and creative needs and experiences of groups or individuals. Collectively they are a social and historical process that reflects the human development of a specific group or society. The second usage of culture will be in its more restrictive or selective sense, that is, to refer to artistic practices and works such as music, dance, literature, painting, sculpture, theatre, film and new media. The two senses of culture – as a particular way of life and as the arts – are very different but are also inter-related. They are connected in that they are deeply involved in the making and understanding of each other. Much of our way of life is spiritual and abstract and it is through the arts that we attempt to make it physical and embodied. On the other hand, the major content and pleasure that we get from the arts draws on our social and historical experiences as well as our desires for the future. It is important to note that culture (in both its possible meanings) is not fixed or static but is fluid and dynamic as it is always in a state of becoming or developing.

## Enter "the struggle"

This section will confine itself to interventions and examples that fall under the broad definition of culture as a way of life. The role of the arts will be considered in the following section.

Many activists and thinkers such as Amilcar Cabral, Frantz Fanon and Bantu Stephen Biko repeatedly argued that the national struggles for liberation across the African continent were in themselves also cultural acts. They meant that if we accept that culture is the totality of a people's self-definition, development and independence, it then follows that the struggle for freedom will express itself through culture in its social, material and creative forms. Conversely, for colonialism to achieve its subjugation of people it is not adequate only to subdue them physically. The minds of the oppressed must also be colonised. This is achieved by denigrating and erasing their culture and replacing it with the ideas, languages, education, arts, architecture and statues that celebrate the culture of the coloniser. An examination of youth and student culture in the fight against apartheid since 1967 will show the validity of such a view. Today, interventions such as #RhodesMustFall indicate an awareness of the politics of culture and the need to decolonise many facets of South African society.

Arguably, one of the best examples of the interconnectedness and mutual influence of the two senses of culture defined above is the toyi-toyi. While the use of song and dance as part of political marches and rallies is a long-standing tradition in South Africa, and variants of the toyi-toyi formed part of the liberation struggle in Zimbabwe, the particular emergence of the toyi-toyi in the 1970s is a unique development that can be attributed to the youth and their cultural innovations. At the obvious level, there is a strong theatrical quality to the toyi-toyi. It is performative in nature. It uses onomatopoeic chanting, call and response and singing. The singing and chanting is accompanied by rhythmic clapping of hands or the high-rise stepping of feet. The body is also used as a canvas. It is adorned with clothing that is inscribed with slogans and it carries symbolic props such as replicas of weapons, coffins and other metaphoric objects. Yet, the toyi-toyi is much more then a theatrical spectacle. Its favoured site of performance is not the stage but public spaces such as streets, courts and other areas that are regarded as the places of officialdom. Since, under apartheid, oppositional groups were prohibited from holding meetings and rallies, other occasions such as marches and funerals were transformed into occasions of mobilisation, conscientisation and resistance. In such cases the toyi-toyi formed part of the battle over public spaces and ideas between the apartheid state and oppositional groups. Furthermore, then and now, the toyi-toyi is a visual, performative and public act of defiance. It was a form of armour that demonstrated the refusal by the oppressed to give in to fear and it instilled individual and collective courage to continue to resist until victory was attained.

Another area of crucial concern that preoccupied students under the banner of SASO (South African Students' Organisation), and young people in general, was the negative portrayal of black people under segregation and, later, apartheid. In order to justify the ideas of white superiority and black inferiority, white supremacists dismissed blacks as unintelligent, primitive, lazy and ugly (to name only a few of the favoured derogatory caricatures). The role and status of blacks in society was always seen as a problem, hence blacks were discussed in the apartheid parliament and in the white community as "the native problem". The caricature of blacks as blank slates led to them being designated "non-whites". This meant that they did not possess any presence or identity of their own and could only be recognised to the extent that they were seen as representing all things bad and opposite to the supposed virtues, intelligence, development and beauty of whites.

In response, SASO and other groups of young people not only challenged the racist stereotypes of the apartheid government but, just as importantly, they engaged in various processes of self-examination and self-definition. They were concerned with whether, as young blacks, they were complicit in seeing themselves in negative terms and behaving in ways that indicated their lack of self-respect, self-belief and dignity. Part of the results of such forms of self-evaluation compelled black youth to acknowledge that they had the agency (however limited) to bring about the changes that they wanted and they should not expect them to be delivered by the very forces that were dominating and exploiting them. Another important recognition was that there were many practices where blacks were conducting themselves in ways that showed they were suffering from inferiority complexes. This required that they seize the initiative in defining, among many other things, who they were and what they aspired to.

Arguably, one of the most crucial interventions made was in the realm of self-definition. The nonsensical term "non-white" was jettisoned and replaced with the proud declaration of blackness and black consciousness as "an attitude of mind, a way of life". Black was not used in terms of skin colour but to refer to all people who were historically oppressed, that is, persons from groups designated "African", so-called "coloureds" and "persons of Indian descent". This sense of black and blackness is currently lost. At the moment we are under the leadership of the new black elites who, in order to secure their self-interests, seem intent on setting the poor and marginal to fight among themselves for meagre resources. This has resulted in the tendency, by some, to distinguish different variations of being black and poor. So now we have "black blacks" and even the "poorest of the poor".

The pride in being black expressed itself in statements such as "black is beautiful". While some may regard the assertion as being trite and a borrowing from the Civil Rights Movement in the USA, one should not underestimate its political, psychological and cultural significances. The statement called on black people to be at ease with and accept the varied ranges of their bodies, whether it be their hair, pigmentation or body shape and size. This meant that white bodies and minds did not have a monopoly on, for instance, beauty and intelligence. In response, the self-styling of young black bodies underwent a number of changes, which were all profound affirmations of African culture and assertive self-pride. Hair straightening and the use of skin lightening creams were frowned upon since they were seen as signs of aspiring to whiteness. Contemporary arguments and terms such as "coconut" and "yellowbone" are, in their own way, a revisiting of the previous debates. Instead natural hair, afros and braids became the norm. The wearing of dashikis, beads, bracelets and accessories derived from or associated with Africa became vogue. Interestingly, it is worth mentioning that the likes of Miriam Makeba and Nina Simone (then fairly young themselves), were pioneers in this regard. In the early 1960s, before the Civil Rights Movement in the USA, artists such as Makeba and Simone were well on the way to being at ease with their blackness without closing themselves off (in terms of languages, musical styles and fashion) to the rest of the world. Theatre groups including Theatre Council of Natal (TECON), Dashiki and People's Experimental Theatre (PET), performed original works such as Mthuli Shezi's *Shanti* and *Black Images* (a collaborative work) and produced plays drawn from the Caribbean and African-American repertoires such as Aime Césaire's *Return to my Native Land* and William Mackay's *Requiem for Brother X*. Bands such as Spirits Rejoice, Malopoets, Africa and Tou fused African rhythms with those of reggae, jazz and soul. A similar attitude towards identity and innovation can be seen in many of the young black musicians and fashion designers currently making waves.

## Performing radical power

Major social upheavals and changes are often preceded by a flourishing of the arts. This is true with regards to South Africa and the years before June 1976. Between 1957 and 1966 dozens of South African artists left the country on exit permits (meaning that they were barred from returning) as the apartheid regime increased its acts of repression that included the banning of the liberation movements in 1960. The arts movements had to find new inspiration and ways of existing. Signs of innovation, especially among the youth, were noticeable towards the end of the 1960s. A major impetus was the rise of the Black Consciousness movement and the formation of SASO. SASO had a Cultural Committee and it invited creative groups to perform at its events. The outlawing of multi-racial events and performances, coupled with the increased repression, had unintended consequences. It created a social context that was receptive to radical interventions. Also, unlike in the 1950s when black artists performed in the cities, the implementation of segregation fostered the possibilities for blacks artists to engage primarily with black audiences in the townships. As mentioned in relation to the toyi-toyi, the bannings and exile of activists and events foregrounded the arts as one of the few terrains where political mobilisation and conscientisation could be pursued. It is no wonder that at the SASO/BPC (Black People's Convention) trial of 1975, the accused were charged with, among other things, conspiring to 'make, produce, publish or distribute subversive and anti-white utterances, writings, poems, plays and/or dramas'.[1]

The popularity of the arts can also be seen in the emergence of arts magazines such as *S'ketsh* (a magazine for popular theatre and entertainment, which appeared intermittently from 1972 to 1979) and *Staffrider* (which appeared intermittently from 1978 to 1998). These magazines aided the cultural revival because they provided platforms for its expression and critical appreciation. The format and layouts of the magazines were experimental and paralleled the creative practices and energies that they engaged with. A typical issue of *Staffrider* included poetry, drama, prose, art, photography, photojournalism, feature articles, interviews and reviews.

The close proximity and synergies between artists and audiences also shifted the tone and style of a lot of work across various genres. In effect, most shows became multi-genre occasions that were held together by the centrality of performance. The young artists were equally diverse in their sources and influences. Some preferred a return to elements associated with indigenous performance traditions and repertoires while others were drawn to the literature, music and theatre produced by African-Americans. Many drew from both traditions. A typical show foregrounded a potent mix of visual, sonic and sensory qualities. It would include a theatrical piece (itself infused with song and movement/dance), music and dance, and readings of poetry and prose. The combination of different genres was also reflected in the composition of the groups. Whatever the artists' preferred creative genre, groups such as Mhloti Black Theatre, MDALI (Music, Drama, Arts and Literature Institute), PET, TECON, Soweto Arts Association (SOARTA) and the Federated Union of Black Artists (FUBA) were in essence incubators for young creatives who dabbled in more than one art form.

Ingoapele Madingoane, an artist and youth of '76, is a good example of one of these multi-disciplinary creatives who deserves greater recognition. Madingoane was a member of Mhloti and MDALI and is the poet who wrote the anthemic *Africa my beginning*. The poem drew on traditional praise or heroic poetry in its form and rendition and was banned soon after its publication in 1979. Madingoane and the poem began to gain notoriety from around 1973. Dressed with African robes slung over his shoulder and having uncombed hair, Madingoane was a mesmerising performer, often accompanied by flute and African percussion. Whether on stage or moving among the audience, he measured and held the epic poem together and the attention of the audience through the repetition of its core refrain, 'Africa my beginning, Africa my end'. In line with the Pan-Africanist visions of the time, the poem mentions the first presidents of the frontline states – Robert Mugabe (Zimbabwe) and Agostinho Neto (Angola), and Namibian struggle stalwart Andimba Herman Toivo ya Toivo – as part of its emphasis that the people and struggles of the continent are one. Young and old South Africans would do well to recall and honour such perspectives and, whatever our local challenges are, not vent our frustrations (and even worse, deadly violence) on fellow Africans. Madingoane and other brilliant and insurgent performance poets and playwrights of the time such as Lefifi Tladi, Matsemela Manaka, Maishe Maponya, Maropodi Mapalakanye and Mzwakhe Mbuli are the poetic predecessors of later wordsmith masters such as Lesego Rampolokeng, Kgafela oa Magogodi, Lebo Mashile and many of the spoken-word poets of today.

The decade also bequeathed many writers who were to become stellar artists. In the area of writing and drama a partial list must include Molefe Phetoe, Mongane Wally Serote, Gladys Thomas, Mafika Gwala, Nomsisi Kraai, Fatima Dike, Chris van Wyk and Gcina Mhlophe. Among fine artists Ben Arnold, Thami Mnyele, Fikile Magadlela and Mpe Figlan come to mind. On the musical front there was an equally startling range of musical groups, styles and content ranging from mbaqanga and progressive jazz to afro-rock. A selective list of the times would include Drive, Soul Brothers, Harari, Steve Kekana, Babs Mlangeni and Sakhile. In spite of the varied nature of their music what appealed to their audiences was the promotion of black pride and creative achievement. A similar tribute can be paid to musical forms that are driven by youth such as kwaito and motswako rappers. Whatever the continuing poverty and marginalisation that post-1994 youth face, their songs proclaim their resilience and hopes. They have re-imagined the townships not only as areas of suffering but also as spaces that have moments of being "ghetto fabulous" where affirming values, pleasures and relationships are also present. Similarly, the use of African languages and slang has changed the attitudes of the broader society towards African languages in popular culture.

It would be remiss of me not to mention, in conclusion, that although young women played a significant and extensive role across all the areas of creative work, the significance of their participation has not received the attention that it deserves.

With the possible exception of published literature, women were very much present in creative endeavours, particularly in the performing arts as playwrights, actresses, singers and so on. The problem is the status that they were accorded: they were not afforded enough opportunities to be directors, choreographers or to perform other leadership roles. The paucity of black women artists is not a consequence of the lack of individual interest and talent. It is the result of socio-economic oppression and exploitation and the subordination of women under patriarchal domination.

Today, under the guise of culture (respecting traditional leaders and customary law), the current South African government is intent on passing the Traditional Leadership and Governance Framework Act. If the Act were passed in its current form it would mean that urban and rural blacks would be treated differently. Rural people, women in particular, would be denied many of their rights as citizens. Then there are the public debates about whether the country is ready to have a woman president. These developments are reminders of the varying roles that culture can play in our personal and social lives. There are those who view culture as beliefs and practices that are inherited complete and unchangeable from the past and there are those who regard culture as dynamic and open to change in response to our hopes of creating a more equal, just and humane world. Depending on your view, culture – whether as a way of life or as "the arts" – can either enslave or liberate.

## Endnotes

1    Attorney General's Report: Documentary exhibits, charge sheet and other materials for the "Treason Trial", 1975, 4.

Bhekizizwe Peterson is professor of African Literature at the University of the Witwatersrand. He has been active in the arts since the 1970s and is the screenplay writer of the feature films *Fools* (1997), *Zulu Love Letter* (Wits University Press, 2009) and *Zwelidumile* (2010).

# CHAPTER 3

# THE ROLE OF RELIGION AND THEOLOGY IN THE ORGANISATION OF STUDENT ACTIVISTS[1]

## IAN MACQUEEN

S outh Africa is, and has long been, deeply religious. From the middle of the 1970s most people in South Africa were nominally members of various Christian denominations. Parts of South Africa experienced some of the most intensive missionary activity anywhere in the world. This rendered both a sizeable class of converted Africans, known as the *amaKholwa* in Natal, as well as breakaway, black-led churches that were known as Ethiopian churches, and which often meshed the new Christian gospel with elements of traditional African religion. Due to the dominance of Christianity in South Africa, it will be our primary focus in this chapter.

Until the apartheid government rolled out Bantu Education in 1954, Christian mission schools such as Healdtown and Lovedale College in the Eastern Cape, and Adams College and St Francis College in KwaZulu-Natal, were the primary educational avenue available to black South Africans. Whereas many churches decided to cede their schools to the government on the commencement of Bantu Education, others did not, and these remained very significant spaces in the schooling of black South Africans.

From the 1960s, religion took on an added significance for students as a covert language for engaging in political discussions, and churches became vital spaces of discussion and contact, as this chapter will discuss. This was because the apartheid government banned all black political parties after the Sharpeville Massacre of 21 March 1960 and other avenues for the discussion of political grievances were closed. The cumulative effect of government repression was to lay a pall of fear on the country that it took the period leading up to 1976 to overcome.

The significance of theology to the struggle was partly because apartheid was a doctrine propounded with a theological rationale. In this understanding, God was seen as the "Great Divider" who had ordained that there be distinct cultures and races. Apartheid, supposedly "separate but equal", was the solution to maintaining each culture separately and thus ensuring God's will was satisfied. As such, apartheid had to be challenged theologically as well as politically. As we will see, theology was a deeply integral part of the language of student organisations in South Africa before the Soweto Uprising of June 1976.

## Changing currents in religion

The 1960s and 1970s were decades of profound change in international Christian organisations like the World Council of Churches (WCC), and the World Student Christian Federation (WSCF). The Roman Catholic Church had initiated long-awaited liberalising changes after the Second Vatican Council of 1962 to 1965, such as allowing for increasing dialogue between Catholics and Christians of other denominations, and indeed others of different faiths. In 1970 the World Council of Churches announced that it would be providing funding to organisations that were fighting racism in different parts of the world, which, significantly, included African liberation organisations such as FRELIMO in Mozambique and the African National Congress (ANC) in South Africa. This move split churches worldwide but also forced them to take very decisive stands. In South Africa churches were divided. The church historian John de Gruchy recalls one synod meeting where a white pastor spoke against the WCC funding, mentioning that his son was serving with the South African army, to which a black pastor countered that his nephew was in fact part of a liberation army that would stand to benefit from the grants.[2]

These international changes also meant increased pressure on South Africa's Student Christian Association (SCA), initially founded in 1896 and then revived following the South African War in 1902, to take a definite stand against apartheid, which it had initially resisted doing. In 1965 when the SCA was called by the WSCF to condemn apartheid, it refused and instead chose to splinter into four ethnically- or language-based groups, namely Bantu, coloured, Afrikaans and English.

## Tracing key religious organisations in the 1960s and 1970s

Both the Anglican and Catholic Churches had affiliated student organisations, namely the Anglican Students' Federation (ASF) and the National Catholic Federation of Students (NCFS), which were racially integrated and which functioned as networks linking students, especially black students at the new so-called "bush colleges" set up under Bantu Education.

Some, however, still saw the need for an integrated, non-denominational Christian movement. When the SCA splintered in 1965, immediate steps were taken by university chaplains, as well the Archbishop of Cape Town, Robert Selby-Taylor, to form a replacement organisation that would be non-racial as the SCA had been. Selby-Taylor called for a meeting of Anglican, Roman Catholic, Methodist, Presbyterian and Congregational Church representatives in Cape Town in November 1966, to discuss the possibility of a new student movement. In July 1967 they launched the new University Christian Movement (UCM) in Grahamstown.

The UCM, under the leadership of Basil Moore, a Methodist minister and academic at Rhodes University, and Colin Collins, a Catholic priest who had been national chaplain to the NCFS, very quickly showed itself to be daring in pushing the boundaries of faith, race and gender norms. It was more attuned to the type of changes sweeping the religious world, mentioned above. It quickly attracted controversy for its radically different approaches to communion/mass, which attracted wild rumours in the press and brought about a negative reputation for the organisation. The UCM attracted a large number of black students, who came to be the majority in the organisation. This was remarkable given that the number of black students in tertiary education in South Africa was tiny in comparison to white students at the time (5 105 black students were enrolled at universities in 1967 compared to 67 294 white students). At a UCM conference at Stutterheim in the Eastern Cape in July 1968, a group of black students broke away to discuss the formation of a blacks-only organisation. They met again at St Francis's College in Mariannhill, KwaZulu-Natal, in December 1968, and launched the South African Students' Organisation (SASO) in July 1969 at the University of the North, Turfloop.

Although black students had initially used the UCM to come together, they later criticised its multiracial approach as the philosophy of Black Consciousness began to take shape. The new discourse asserted a "black and proud" way of life that blacks should embrace to liberate themselves and viewed multiracialism as a dead end. As black students pulled out of the UCM, the founding churches cut their funding to the organisation as allegations of irregularities and even of heresy, an unacceptable distortion of doctrine, grew against the student group. The government set up a secret commission of enquiry, under Alwyn Schlebusch, to investigate the organisation. As a result of these pressures, the UCM disbanded in 1972.

In the aftermath, other organisations needed to step in to fill the space. Although the SCA had split in 1965 along racial lines, it still continued to play a role, particularly among high school pupils. The historian Clive Glaser notes the importance of the student Christian movements as spaces where students could engage in political discussions in Soweto prior to 1976, calling these groups 'crucial early incubators of political ideas and student leadership'.[3]

The Anglican Students' Federation also escaped government repression, as did the National Catholic Federation of Students, though black students quit the organisation in 1971. Although the NCFS lost direct black support, it became a key space in which Albert Nolan, a Dominican monk who taught theology at the University of Stellenbosch and who was the national chaplain of the NCFS, began to develop a liberation theology that drew from South America. The NCFS had drawn from radical South American theologians such as Hélder Câmara, Camilo Torres and Hugo Assmann from at least as early as the mid-1960s. The newsletter of the organisation, *Katutura*, a Herero word meaning "we have no permanent resting place here", that is also the name of a township in current-day Namibia, published excerpts of the South American theologians' writings, and the editors drew simple analogies with the South African situation. *Katutura* was thus an early avenue for the influence of this theology on South African students. The national conferences of the NCFS were also deeply influenced by Liberation Theology. Albert Nolan refined these comparisons, and his lectures to the NCFS national conferences, which would later form the basis of his book *Jesus before Christianity*, published in 1976, drew particular attention to the socio-political context of Jesus' life and emphasised his solidarity with the poor and downtrodden. Although both Liberation Theology and Black Theology drew attention to the plight of the oppressed, they had different origins and avenues of development, as we will shortly see with the story of the emergence of Black Theology in South Africa.

## The role of religion and theology

A key theological development in South Africa was the marrying of the idea of political liberation to a traditional understanding of Christian liberation. The Gospel promised liberation from sin and eternal life to those who surrender their hearts to Christ. Some theologians began to take this further, arguing that this liberation should include freedom from oppression, particularly under apartheid, and to see Christ not only as guaranteeing eternal life, but also as being concerned with temporal liberation. In this sense, the Bible became a site of contestation, with apartheid theologians drawing from it to support their doctrine, whereas activists would increasingly claim it as a document of liberation. A text which quoted Jesus at the start of his public ministry in his hometown of Nazareth, taken from the prophet Isaiah, became key:

> The Spirit of the Lord is upon me, because he has anointed me to proclaim good news to the poor. He has sent me to proclaim liberty to the captives and recovering of sight to the blind, to set at liberty those who are oppressed to proclaim the year of the Lord's favour.

> Luke 4:18-19, English Standard Version

The key phrases 'liberty to the captives', and 'to set at liberty those who are oppressed', were vital hooks upon which this new theology hung its claim to political liberation on the basis of the Gospel. Another component was reclaiming the confidence that God had created black people out of His good will, in complete equality and not to be forever 'hewers of wood and drawers of water', as Hendrik Verwoerd had once claimed.

The changes in theology arguably had some of their roots in the 1960s as well. The world was perceived at the time as becoming increasingly secular, as science seemed to be replacing God. The scientific and engineering feats of sending humans into space and landing them on the moon appeared to imply that humankind had finally come of age and could throw off its "superstitions". Some theologians responded by embracing the secular as a fulfilment of God's will. These debates found their way into South Africa, where they began to feed into students' discussions about what it meant to be a Christian and what the Gospel fundamentally meant for their time. These ideas were particularly prominent in the UCM.

The UCM in South Africa established contact with James Cone, an American theologian and foremost proponent of Black Theology. They sent Basil Moore and two black students to the University Christian Movement conference in Cleveland, Ohio, in December 1967, where Moore was persuaded to meet with James Cone, who would later teach at Union Theological Seminary. At the meeting in New York City, Cone gave Moore an advance copy of his book *Black Theology and Black Power*, which was published in 1969. Their meeting and Cone's book influenced Moore to pen an essay on his return to South Africa, titled *Towards a Black Theology*, which he presented at UCM seminars around the country. In the essay, Moore drew a direct comparison between the situation of blacks in South Africa and the Jews of Jesus' day under Roman occupation. He argued that it was only 'where the Church stands identified' with 'the poor, dehumanised, enslaved and politically disinherited people' that it could deserve 'to be called the Church'.[4]

Moore's visit to the United States, and the seminars he presented, led to the UCM establishing a Black Theology Project under the charge of Sabelo Stanley Ntwasa (Robert Sobukwe's nephew), a student at the Federal Theological Seminary (FEDSEM). The ideas of Black Theology immediately found a receptive ear among the black clergy. The South African Students' Organisation also endorsed Black Theology. Steve Biko, SASO's first president and later chair of SASO Publications, recognised that anyone wishing to influence the African community who neglected the importance of religion, would be destined to fail, and thus he attempted to establish connections with black clergy. A sign of the success of Black Theology, and its early adoption by the best of a new crop of intellectuals, was the publication of a collection of essays in 1972, titled *Essays on Black Theology*, which was edited by Ntwasa, but appeared under the name of Mokgethi Motlhabi, due to a banning order on Ntwasa, which prevented him from publishing material, among other restrictions.

A significant outcome of the Black Theology Project and the UCM's own experimentation, was that it presented activists with a way in which Christianity and faith could be adapted to speak to pressing, immediate issues. When the apartheid government became aware of the danger that SASO and Black Consciousness posed, it began a campaign of harassment and intimidation against the people involved. Mthuli Shezi, an activist from the University of Zululand, was among the first to be killed when he was pushed in front of a train in Germiston for opposing the bad treatment of black women. Abram Tiro was the next to die, assassinated in Gaborone by a parcel bomb, possibly sent by a South African Special Branch police unit. The deaths of Shezi and Tiro, both fervent Christians, came to be seen as a form of martyrdom, explained and described using Christian imagery. As the state moved more forcefully to curb the activities of SASO, so activists relied on the resources of a new-found belief, derived from Christianity, which the historian Daniel Magaziner describes as 'a political faith'.[5]

For activists who had deep faith, politics and religion could never be separated, as each informed the other. If apartheid was justified using biblical rationale, their opposition to the government also rested on a particular reading of the Bible. Activists would later look back on this shift in thinking as a second "conversion" experience. Frank Chikane, at the time a student at the University of the North, described his exposure to Black Theology as '[unleashing] in me energies and commitments I never knew were there. It enabled me to engage in political action as a Christian … It brought me into the struggle'.[6]

## A closer look at some individuals

The significance of religion and theology can be discerned in some of the dominant personalities of the Black Consciousness movement. Steve Biko attended two of the historic mission schools mentioned earlier, Lovedale College near Alice in the Eastern Cape and St Francis College near Pinetown in Natal. Before becoming widely known as the face of the Black Consciousness movement, he began a correspondence with Aelred Stubbs, an Anglican monk belonging to the Community of the Resurrection. In letters to Stubbs, Biko expressed his concern, among other matters, about Christian doctrine. This interest is openly evident in his later writings, particularly *The Church as Seen by a Young Layman*, in the collection of his writings *I Write what I Like*, compiled by Stubbs after Biko's death. In the essay, which he presented to black clergymen, Biko argued that Christianity was too closely linked to European culture and had been corrupted to suit apartheid and keep blacks subservient.

Barney Pityana was Biko's fellow SASO leader. Their association began early when they shared a desk at Lovedale College. Pityana was a deeply committed Christian who was president of the Anglican Students' Federation in 1968, the year that black students began to form SASO. Stubbs also befriended Pityana, embarking on what he would later call an 'extended ministry … of a personal and unofficial nature' to the leaders of the Black Consciousness movement.[7] It is clear here that for Biko, Pityana and Stubbs, their religious life informed and was shaped by their political involvements.

As we have seen, Frank Chikane described being "converted" to a Black Theology perspective. He was the son of an Apostolic Faith Mission (AFM) preacher and came to politics through an initial involvement in the Student Christian Movement. He was exposed to Black Theology ideas while a student at the University of the North, Turfloop, a campus where SASO was particularly strong. While he retained his membership in the Apostolic Faith Mission, which discouraged involvement in politics, Chikane's exposure to Black Theology and Black Consciousness ensured that he was very active politically, resulting in his being arrested and tortured by the police and being defrocked as a minister of the AFM.

Albert Nolan, like Collins before him, was a national chaplain to the NCFS. Born in Cape Town in 1934, he joined the Dominican Order and taught theology in Stellenbosch in the 1960s. His capacity as national chaplain allowed Nolan to travel around the country and attend conferences internationally. Although the NCFS lost its black constituency, the organisation moved very far in adopting a radical critique of apartheid. Nolan emerged as the proponent of a particular form of South African Liberation Theology, which asserted God's solidarity with the poor and oppressed, 'the preferential option for the poor'.[8]

## Connecting faith to politics

While we can speak of a secular and a spiritual, it is evident that this was not such a defined distinction for many activists – commitment to one spilled over and informed the other. It is also clear that student Christian organisations played the role of integrating and bringing individuals together, whereas apartheid sought to drive them apart. Furthermore, these organisations provided connections to the outside world – Moore's visit to the UCM conference in the USA and subsequent meeting with Cone, is an example. Lastly, these organisations provided vital spaces that allowed discussion of the realities people were facing, and groomed future leaders. These roles all took on added significance in the absence of legal representative political parties.

At the same time, theology was informed by people's experience, and was drawn on to strengthen people's commitment to the struggle against apartheid. Apartheid was increasingly criticised from a theological, as well as an ethical, position. This was crystallised in the publication of the Kairos Document in 1985, which called for Christians to participate in the struggle against apartheid. By bringing together their faith and their activism, activists were able to derive strength from their faith, and a rationale for the great personal costs many had to pay. The Soweto Uprising represented a victory over the fear that had characterised the previous decade. A component of this victory was the aligning of faith with activism. In 1976, the same year as the Soweto Uprising and the year that Nolan published *Jesus before Christianity*, Allan Boesak, a pastor of the coloured branch of the Dutch Reformed Church in Paarl, published his doctoral thesis, *Farewell to Innocence*, the first systematic exploration of Black Theology from a South African perspective. The book captured the popular shift that had taken place in the 1970s. Black Theology grew increasingly academic after this, as black theological students returned from doctoral studies abroad. Together, these represented the consolidation of the powerful changes that had occurred in the preceding decade.

# Endnotes

1   This chapter draws from my PhD thesis, Reimaging South Africa: Black Consciousness, Radical Christianity and the New Left, 1967–1977, University of Sussex, 2011, and subsequent research conducted between 2013 and 2015, funded by a National Research Foundation Innovation Postdoctoral award.

2   J. de Gruchy, *The Church Struggle in South Africa, 2nd Ed.* Cape Town: David Philip, 1986, 136-137.

3   C. Glaser, We must infiltrate the Tsotsis: School politics and youth gangs in Soweto, 1968–1976, *Journal of Southern African Studies*, 1998, 24(2), 303.

4   B. Moore, Towards a Black Theology, Wits Historical Papers (WHP), AD 1126 D69(a), William Cullen Library, University of the Witwatersrand.

5   D. Magaziner, *The Law and the Prophets: Black Consciousness in South Africa, 1968–1977.* Athens: Ohio University Press, 2010.

6   Interview with F. Chikane by B. Moore, cited in Moore, Learning from Black Theology, paper prepared for Rhodes University Graduation, 8 April 2011, Found at: https://www.ru.ac.za/media/rhodesuniversity/content/ruhome/documents/Basil%20Moore%20Speech%20%20-%20Black%20Theology.pdf (accessed on 16 March 2016).

7   Letter from Aelred Stubbs to friends, September 1977, Alphaeus Zulu Papers, 98/3/59 Statements/Papers/Press Releases, Killie Campbell Africana Library, University of KwaZulu-Natal, Durban.

8   A. Nolan, *Jesus before Christianity*. London: Longman and Todd, 1977.

Ian Macqueen joined the University of Pretoria in January 2015, where he lectures in the Department of Historical and Heritage Studies. He draws in his chapter in this volume from his PhD thesis, Reimaging South Africa: Black Consciousness, Radical Christianity and the New Left, 1967–1977 (University of Sussex, 2011).

# CHAPTER 4

# STUDENT ORGANISATION IN LEHURUTSHE AND THE IMPACT OF ONKGOPOTSE ABRAM TIRO

ARIANNA LISSONI

A village called Dinokana, near the town of Zeerust in what is today South Africa's North West Province (formerly the western Transvaal), is the birthplace of one of the most important leaders of the Black Consciousness movement, Onkgopotse Abram Tiro. Although he was tragically assassinated by a parcel bomb in February 1974, in Botswana, where he had gone into exile, Tiro had a profound influence on student politics in South Africa, and the development of Black Consciousness (BC) ideology and its affiliated organisations, under whose broad banner the youth of 1976 mobilised.

Tiro is remembered for his leadership role in a number of Black Consciousness organisations (SASO, SASM and BCP) and, perhaps most importantly, for a speech he gave at Turfloop's graduation ceremony in 1972, for which he was expelled from the university. In this famous speech, Tiro openly attacked the white and Bantustan authorities present at the ceremony as well as apartheid's Bantu Education system.[1] Tiro's expulsion was a historical turning point as it inspired a series of solidarity protests in black campuses across the country, marking the embrace of confrontational action by SASO that was to culminate in the "Viva FRELIMO" rallies of 1974.

The focus of this essay is on lesser known aspects of Tiro's life[2] – the rural world that made him, and the significant links that he retained with this world, particularly through mentoring younger generations of students from Lehurutshe, where Dinokana is located. Lehurutshe is a rural area stretching approximately 100 kilometres along the Botswana border north of the town of Zeerust. It was one of South Africa's native reserves (known as Moiloa's Reserve) and became part of the Bophuthatswana Bantustan during the apartheid era, until its reincorporation into South Africa in 1994.

While the 1976 student uprisings have been fairly well documented in Johannesburg's townships and black urban townships elsewhere, particularly on the Rand, the development of student politics in the large expanses of South Africa's countryside has been overlooked in historical accounts of the 1976 unrest and its origins. Rural politics, including student and youth politics, often tends to be viewed as derivative of events and actions taking place in the country's major cities, where political agency appears to originate, while local political dynamics and concerns rooted in the deep histories of localities, which give particular form and content to resistance on the ground elsewhere, are ignored. This essay thus seeks to understand youth resistance and organisation in the countryside through a local historical lens, and not just in terms of the Soweto Uprising spreading to and reverberating in one direction from urban to rural contexts. As the essay will argue, the relationship between urban and rural struggles over time needs to be re-thought in more complex terms.

## The Hurutshe revolt

Tiro began his schooling at Ikalafeng Primary School in Dinokana in the early 1950s, but the school was closed as a result of the violence that engulfed Lehurutshe from 1957 to 1959. The immediate impetus for the Hurutshe revolt, also known as the Zeerust Uprising, was the imposition of Bantu Authorities[3] and the introduction of passes for women.[4] Because of his refusal to comply with the authorities on these issues, the Dinokana *kgosi*, Abram Ramotshere Moiloa, was deposed and had to escape to the Bechuanaland Protectorate (today Botswana) to avoid political banning to the Victoria East District in the Cape Province.[5] The period of protracted resistance that ensued was met by severe state repression through mass arrests, fines, political bannings and persecution by the police, with the help of collaborationist chiefs and their militias. Like other instances of rural rebellion taking place around this period (for example in Sekhukhuneland and Pondoland), the Hurutshe resistance was also linked to the national urban-based movements through migrant workers and their associations. In February 1958, two years prior to its nation-wide banning, the African National Congress (ANC) was outlawed in the area, and hundreds of villagers were displaced as a result of the violence.

The Hurutshe revolt had a major impact on the conscientisation of successive generations of young people growing up in Lehurutshe, as the memory of the violence suffered during this period left many with a strong sense of injustice. According to Dikgang Uhuru Moiloa, who was born in Dinokana in 1958 in the midst of the upheaval:

> [A]ll of us knew what had happened in our village [Dinokana], there was no student of my time of my age who did not have a sense of what had happened in the village and why the chief [Abram Moiloa] had to go into exile for 18 years. We knew. We grew up knowing why the chief was in exile. So there was a general political consciousness in the village even though it was heavily suppressed [by the apartheid state].[6]

The arrests and trials of the period 1957–59 also left many children with no means of material support. During this period, young Tiro variously worked in a manganese mine, as a dishwasher, and as a general labourer,[7] until he was able to resume his schooling, first at Naledi High in Soweto and then at Barolong High in Mafikeng (which was then one of the few schools in the country that prepared black students for university training), where he matriculated. The suppression of the rural rebellions by the apartheid state in this period laid the ground for the establishment of a new political order in the South African countryside, that of the Bantustans (or "homelands"). This brought to an effective end the remaining political autonomy of the remnants of pre-colonial African chiefdoms, as Bantu Authorities turned chiefs into salaried officials of the apartheid state. This period also marked the final destruction of traditional African peasant economies, which had been under transformation as a result of colonial and capitalist penetration since at least the late nineteenth century.

The events of the late 1950s in Lehurutshe, and more generally his rural upbringing, certainly shaped Tiro's politics, especially with regards to the centrality of the land question to African political and economic independence. He argued that 'the primary source of income for blacks is land, and we need to restore land to the dispossessed'.[8] The Bantustan system became one of the key targets of the Black Consciousness movement – Steve Biko called the Bantustans 'the greatest single fraud ever invented by white politicians'.[9]

Because of its proximity to the border and the historic and kinship ties of the Bahurutshe with neighbouring Botswana, Lehurutshe also became a key node in the

ANC underground machinery set up in the early 1960s, acting as a gateway for political activists going into exile and for Umkhonto we Sizwe (MK) recruits slipping out of the country for military training.[10] It also became an important recruiting ground for MK, to which it contributed a newly-initiated *mophato* or age regiment of between fifty and eighty young men and boys. Because of their young age, the recruits from Lehurutshe were nicknamed *mmaguerrilla a nnete*, or MK's "true guerrillas".

## Abram Tiro and student organisation in Lehurutshe

After matriculation, Tiro enrolled at the University of the North, Turfloop, and was elected president of the Student Representative Council (SRC) in 1970. At the time of his expulsion from Turfloop in 1972, he was also involved in the formation of the South African Students' Movement (SASM), of which he was elected president in 1973, and of the Black People's Convention (BPC). In that year he also took over as SASO's permanent organiser after a spate of bannings incapacitated much of the Black Consciousness leadership, including Steve Biko. While SASO primarily mobilised students based at tertiary institutions, SASM's role was to organise secondary school students. For this purpose Tiro travelled throughout South Africa, as well as in Botswana, Swaziland and Lesotho, to speak to students about Black Consciousness.

The apartheid authorities, however, were soon to close down on Tiro. First they had him fired from Morris Isaacson High School in Soweto where he was teaching. Then, in late 1973 when it became clear that he would be arrested, Tiro was forced to move to Botswana. He found employment as a teacher at a school in Kgale, near Gaborone. On 1 February 1974, he was killed by a parcel bomb allegedly coming from the International University Exchange Fund (IUEF) in Switzerland. Tiro was among the first victims of cross-border attacks by an apartheid hit squad known as the "Z squad". The TRC was unable to establish the exact circumstances of Tiro's murder, as no one claimed responsibility for it.[11] In 1998 Tiro's remains were exhumed from Botswana and reburied in his home village of Dinokana by AZAPO. During his short life Tiro was able to touch the lives of many young people thus planting 'the seed of what was to be the 1976 uprising'.[12]

Among the new generation of activists from the western Transvaal that Tiro inspired was Zachariah (Zakes) Pitso Tolo, who was brought up by his grandmother in

Lekubu (Braklaagte), another village in Lehurutshe, while both of his parents worked in Johannesburg. While growing up, he used to listen to his grandmother and other women in the village tell stories about:

> the days of the Boers, … Strydom, and the anti-pass campaign … And we
> were also taught not to talk about these things because should people hear,
> you know, other people that were working for the system, they would
> know that this particular household is sympathetic [to the ANC]. That's
> when we were taught secrecy, we were taught not to talk about sensitive
> issues. But this contributed greatly to our conscientisation.[13]

The only secondary school in the vicinity was in the village of Motswedi. Zakes Tolo remembers that while he was studying at Motswedi Secondary, Abram Tiro would come and engage with students in Lehurutshe during the school holidays. Tiro would meet the students in small groups 'to discuss issues around education, the type of problems we faced, the need for us to participate in sporting activities, … to create study groups at school and so forth'. This was 'more of an orientation, political education type of thing, it was not yet a[n organised] resistance movement', but it provided a foundation for political mobilisation by starting to 'develop a sense of Black Consciousness, [and] pride in ourselves'.[14]

Following in Tiro's footsteps, Zakes Tolo went on to study at Barolong High School in Mafikeng. When he was expelled from Turfloop in 1972, Tiro went to Barolong and reported what had happened to the students at the university. Zakes Tolo still vividly remembers what Tiro told them:

> I am here, I have been kicked out of school [Turfloop], I am a member
> of the South African Students' Organisation who are attacking this Bantu
> Education. My crime [is that I] questioned the presence of the white
> people who did not know the graduates and our parents could not even
> attend the graduation ceremony, we are being converted into animals in
> the zoo by these whites who don't even know [how to] pronounce our
> names.

He also encouraged them to study, and added:

> Those of you who are going to Turfloop next year and other universities,
> you must know that these are "bush colleges", [but that] these are also the
> terrain of struggle.[15]

In 1973, Tolo went to study at Turfloop where he enrolled for a Teacher's Diploma
and joined SASO. In this period he interacted with prominent BC activists through
events organised by the SRC, such as Africa Arts Week, which brought radical black
artists and speakers – for example, Don Mattera, Wally Serote, Joe Matthews, and the
musical groups Tashiki and Fifi Tladi – to the university campus. In September 1974,
the SRC/SASO organised one of the pro-FRELIMO rallies that were suppressed by
the state through the banning, arrest and trial of several SASO/BPC leaders, which in
effect rendered these organisations leaderless. In this period the ANC underground
network started to move into the vacuum left by the SASO leadership crisis and established small cells on black campuses such as Turfloop. Tolo was recruited by one of his
Turfloop lecturers, George Mashamba, into an underground unit secretly operating at
the university, which established contact with the ANC in Botswana through people
such as Snuki Zikalala and Keith Mokoape in Gaborone.[16]

Tolo then took up a teaching job at Ga-Rankuwa High School, where he worked
with Victor Sefora, a former secretary general of the ANC Youth League, and the leader
of Seoposengwe Party, the opposition party in Bophuthatswana. This was the base for
another underground cell linked to the ANC Botswana machinery, which was involved
in smuggling arms and propaganda material into South Africa until a police crackdown
in 1977 ultimately forced Tolo into exile.

Dikgang Uhuru Moiloa was another youth from Dinokana who became politicised
through rural student politics in the 1970s and on whom Onkgopotse Tiro made a big
impression. He was at Keobusitse Middle School (in Dinokana), when Tiro addressed
the students about his expulsion from Turfloop:

> He gave us a good political lecture and told us why he was there, why
> he was expelled and why we must stick to education irrespective [of

the injustice of the system of Bantu Education] and he narrated the whole situation about how black people are being treated ... The kind of environment that the black students find themselves in, and what is it that we need to do in order to undo that system. Now that is the education and the lecture that stayed in my mind forever, and in any interview about my life, my biography, I mention this because it is actually the [turning] point.[17]

It was probably around 1973 that the Zeerust African Students' Association (ZASA) was formed by local secondary school students. Tiro had encouraged the rural youth to come together in a students' association for the purpose of 'sharing your experiences, you will be creating synergy to address whatever problem that you have, this institution will again assist you in conducting afternoon studies and if you pick up any problem in any subject you guys must form study groups'.[18]

Initially, ZASA and its related activities were not overtly political. Rather, they focused on issues that were of immediate concerns to students, for example, the setting up of study groups to help them tackle difficult subjects such as Science and Agriculture, which were being taught in Afrikaans. Students also collected money among themselves so that they could buy the *Rand Daily Mail* or the *World* newspapers, which they would read and share. This way, they were able to keep informed about events in the country.

Uhuru Moiloa joined ZASA after starting high school at Dinokana Secondary School and became one of its executive members around 1975. Moiloa credits Zakes Tolo and SASO activists who passed through Lehurutshe as they went into exile with influencing his political make up and his involvement in the organisation. According to Moiloa, before the explosion of the Soweto Uprising in June 1976, ZASA had already independently embarked on a campaign to end corporal punishment at Dinokana Secondary School. In particular, the campaign 'actually demanded that the principal be expelled because he was assaulting kids, particularly girl children'.[19] Although this was a spontaneous and uncoordinated action, the campaign ended up having a significant impact, both in terms of raising the levels of political consciousness of fellow students, and for the Dinokana community at large. Moiloa recalls that the ZASA executive discussed the idea of the campaign during one of its meetings and a decision was taken to embark on action the following day. The next morning, Moiloa and a fellow student called Eric Mothoagae went into the principal's office and removed all the sticks he used to beat the students. When the principal summoned them to his office Moiloa and Mothoagae:

> went class to class, we went door to door in the school mobilising the students to get out of the classrooms ... and in no minute ... we were there raising a matter that was of concern to every school child, every student ... [after] about 30 minutes the whole school was out[side] and people were singing and that was [when] for the first time we started raising a clenched fist ... the Black Consciousness sign of power.[20]

The authorities were called in and the South African Defence Force (SADF) (stationed at the nearby Lobatse border post) entered Dinokana with armoured vehicles and surrounded the school. A small group of about eight students, among them Uhuru Moiloa, were identified as the "ringleaders" of the protest and arrested. This was not the end of it, however. Uhuru Moiloa proudly remembers this was the moment:

> when chief Abram Moiloa [who had returned from exile in Botswana in 1975] showed his true colours as a Congress person ... He came to Zeerust police station the following day and demanded that we be released, you know, and we were released.[21]

After their release, the old *kgosi* addressed the students:

> The chief addressed us and gave us tips that he is part of us, he had stayed 18 years in exile, he knows where the ANC is. The important thing for us is to get educated so that we should be able to lead our people effectively. I mean those words still resonate in my mind even now, you know.[22]

When the students of Soweto rose in June 1976 in protest against being taught in Afrikaans, the period passed relatively quietly in the Lehurutshe area. Uhuru Moiloa explains that:

by 1976 when the Soweto uprisings started, I was a student in Dinokana but we did not riot like everybody else, we were taking it a little bit carefully by that time, we were treading very carefully because we had already had an experience of suppression and they brought in the army [to deal with the students].[23]

In December 1977, Moiloa left Lehurutshe by boarding a train to Johannesburg, where some of his family were based. This was an act of defiance against Bophuthatswana's "independence" celebrations, in which Moiloa was meant to be singing as part of a student choir. He went on to become one of the founding members of the Congress of South African Students (COSAS) in 1979. After his arrest and trial for taking part in a march in honour of Solomon Kalushi Mahlangu, the Umkhonto we Sizwe (MK) cadre executed by the apartheid regime, Moiloa became part of the ANC underground network in the 1980s.[24]

## Conclusion

This essay has provided a brief overview of youth and student involvement in the struggle against apartheid in the period from the late 1950s to the late 1970s, from a rural point of view. One of the conclusions to be drawn from this account is that the tempo of youth and student resistance across rural geographies needs to be understood within the context of their deeper histories and local political dynamics. The Hurutshe revolt of the late 1950s was in many ways a turning point for the history and politics of that part of the country. On one hand it marked the beginning of a new social and political order in the countryside that had been brought under the control of an increasingly interventionist and authoritarian state in a more direct way. On the other hand, and in spite of the suppression of popular resistance by the state, this period of political upheaval remained embedded in the collective subconscious of successive generations of rural youths from the area, thus playing a significant role in the development of their political consciousness and activism. In the aftermath of the rebellion, a cohort of boys and young men from Lehurutshe were recruited into the underground machinery and into MK.

Onkgopotse Tiro, who became one of the most important leaders and thinkers of

Black Consciousness, was directly affected by these events. Although Tiro was killed in 1974, his ideas were influential for the generation of secondary school students who were at the centre of the June 1976 uprising. Moreover, Tiro was central to the political formation of younger students from Dinokana and neighbouring villages in Lehurutshe, like Zakes Tolo and Uhuru Moiloa. Contrary to the general belief that young people in the countryside were politically unsophisticated, they had often achieved a level of political awareness through their own local struggles and activities, as for example those carried out by ZASA. While narratives about the 1976 uprising have primarily focused on Soweto and other urban townships, youth organisation and resistance in the countryside needs to be understood in local terms, and not just as an extension of urban politics.

## Endnotes

1   See graduation speech by Onkgopotse Tiro at the University of the North, 29 April 1972, available at http://www.sahistory.org.za/article/graduation-speech-onkgopotse-tiro-university-north-29-april-1972.

2   For a poetic tribute to Tiro's life see the film documentary *A Blues for Tiro* (2007) by Steve Kwena Mokwena.

3   The Bantu Authorities Act of 1951 had an impact on chiefly authority, sometimes privileging pro-government chiefs over anti-government ones.

4   See C. Hooper, *Brief Authority*. London: Collins, 1960; T. Lodge, *Black Politics in South Africa since 1945*. Johannesburg: Ravan Press, 1983; S. Zondi, Peasant Struggles in the 1950s: GaMatlala and Zeerust, in SADET (ed.), *The Road to Democracy in South Africa, Vol. 1, 1960–1970*. Cape Town: Zebra Press, 2004; J. Fairbairn, Zeerust: A Profile of Resistance, *Africa South*, 1958, 30-38; A. Manson, *The Troubles of Kgosi Abram Moiloa: The Hurutshe Resistance of 1954–1958*. Johannesburg: South African Institute of Race Relations, 1983.

5   See S. Badat, *The Forgotten People: Political Banishment under Apartheid*. Johannesburg: Jacana, 2012.

6   Interview with Dikgang Uhuru Moiloa by Arianna Lissoni, Johannesburg, 2 December 2008.

7   Child labour was then a fairly widespread practice and many black children of Tiro's generation worked on neighbouring white farms, particularly during harvest season.

8   Onkgopotse Tiro quoted in http://www.sahistory.org.za/pages/people/bios/tiro,a.htm.

9   S. Biko, Let's talk about Bantustans, in *I Write what I Like*. A. Stubbs (ed.). London: Heinemann, 1987.

10  Interview with Moumakwa by Suttner, 15 May 2003, available at https://www.aluka.org/struggles/collection/SUTTNR.

11  Truth and Reconciliation Commission, *The Report of the Truth and Reconciliation Commission*, Volume 3, http://www.nelsonmandela.org/omalley/index.php/site/q/03lv021 67/04lv02264/05lv02335/06lv02357/07lv02380/08lv02386.htm.

12  A. Mphaki, Death of godfather of student uprising still a mystery, *The Star*, 2 February 2012.

13  Interview with Zakes Pitso Tolo by Arianna Lissoni, Mafikeng, 26 January 2009.

14  Ibid.

15  Ibid.

16  See Houston and Magubane, The ANC Political Underground in the 1970s, SADET (ed.), *The Road to Democracy in South Africa Vol. 2: 1970–1980*, Pretoria: UNISA Press, 2006, 371-451.

17  Interview with Dikgang Uhuru Moiloa, 2 December 2008.

18  Interview with Zakes Pitso Tolo, by Arianna Lissoni, Mafikeng, 26 January 2009.

19  Interview with Dikgang Uhuru Moiloa, 2 December 2008.

20  Ibid.

21  Ibid.

22  Ibid.

23  Ibid.

24  Interview with Dikgang Uhuru Moiloa by Arianna Lissoni, Johannesburg, 18 March 2009.

Arianna Lissoni is a researcher in the History Workshop at the University of the Witwatersrand. She obtained her PhD, titled The South African Liberation Movements in Exile, c. 1945–1970, from the School of Oriental and African Studies, London, in 2008. She is one of the editors of the *South African Historical Journal* and co-edited the volumes *One Hundred Years of the ANC: Debating liberation histories today* (Wits University Press, 2012) and *The ANC between Home and Exile: Reflections on the anti-apartheid struggle in Italy and Southern Africa* (Università degli studi di Napoli "L'Orientale", 2015). Her research interests are South African liberation history and politics.

CHAPTER 5

# THE UNIVERSITY OF THE NORTH
## A regional and national centre of activism[1]

ANNE HEFFERNAN

T he Extension of University Education Act of 1959 created a system of
universities and colleges across South Africa that were segregated not just
by race, but by ethnic group. One of these, the University College of the
North, was responsible for educating students of Sotho, Tswana, Venda, and Tsonga
backgrounds who, it was imagined, would become the civil servants, doctors, engineers
and other professionals who would populate the surrounding "homelands" of Venda,
Lebowa, Gazankulu, and Bophuthatswana. Instead, "Turfloop", as the University
College of the North was known, became a centre for anti-apartheid political activism
for students and young people around the region of the northern Transvaal (now
Limpopo) and beyond.

Like other so-called "bush colleges" Turfloop was geographically isolated, but
strategically located near several of the homelands in South Africa's rural north. From
1972 it fell technically within the borders of Lebowa, but continued to be administered
by the Department of Bantu Education of South Africa, and to educate students
from other homelands and from urban townships. In its early years this division was
approximately half-and-half, with slightly more students coming from surrounding
rural areas. Over the 1960s, as the population of Turfloop grew significantly (in 1960,
its first class consisted of only 87 students; by the end of the decade, in 1969, it had
630)[2] the balance shifted and urban students outnumbered rural ones.

This chapter explores the years in the late 1960s and early 1970s, when the
university became a national centre for activism through the influence of the South
African Students' Organisation (SASO) and key student activists. It argues that, due to

early permissiveness on the part of university authorities and to the peculiar character of life in an "apartheid university" Turfloop was especially fertile ground for political mobilisation. It suggests that SASO's close relationship to student governance at the university, and its keen organisational capacity, played important roles in driving mobilisation there. It also contends that the political influence of the university was magnified and extended by the expulsion of a number of students who went on to become school teachers, many of them in Soweto during the early 1970s, and then to work in other fields of political organisation.

## The South African Students' Organisation and the transformation of Turfloop

The South African Students' Organisation was founded in December 1968 at the black section of the University of Natal. Its birth was the result of dissatisfaction among some black students about the ability of the existing national student organisation, NUSAS (the National Union of South African Students), to represent the interests of a black constituency.

At Turfloop, SASO had a somewhat variable beginning. Its first national conference was held there in July of 1969, where Steve Biko was elected the organisation's first president. Under the leadership of students Harry Nengwekhulu and Petrus Machaka, the Turfloop Students' Representative Council used its own funds to support the conference, which brought it into conflict with the university registrar who was concerned about SASO's ability to repay the money.[3] But the SRC was entitled to spend its student dues as it saw fit, and from the outset it made a commitment to support SASO not just politically, but financially as well.

SASO's emergence on campus was one in a succession of engagements in national politics by students at Turfloop. They had been disallowed from affiliating with NUSAS in 1968 after a long battle between university officials and the SRC, and the multiracial University Christian Movement was coming under increased pressure from university authorities by the end of the decade. In fact, university administrators at the time encouraged black Turfloop students to form their own organisation rather than be "used" by NUSAS.[4] SASO's on-campus leaders used this to their advantage. They garnered the tacit permission of the university administration for SASO to operate on campus. The formation of an all-black student organisation, instead of the older non-racial national union, aligned neatly with the ideals of separate development, which underlay the founding of the university itself. It also marked a point of intersection – surprisingly, perhaps – between the politics of SASO and the vast majority of white university staff in its anti-white liberal (and by extension, anti-NUSAS) stance.

During this period of relative laxity on the part of the university administration, SASO built a strong presence on campus at Turfloop and at other black campuses throughout South Africa. It did so by holding frequent and regular branch meetings, local formation schools, executive meetings, and annual General Students Councils (GSCs).[5] Branch meetings, on the smallest and most local scale, built up SASO's organisational capacity on individual campuses.

Turfloop became an early bastion of SASO support both politically and monetarily. Affiliation was arranged for the student body as a whole, through the SRC, rather than on an individual membership basis. It was the site of SASO's inaugural congress, and many formation schools were held in surrounding locations, attracting Turfloop students and others from local and regional areas. These were essentially workshops geared at deepening political education for existing SASO members, and extending it to new ones. Such formation schools formed an additional layer of SASO's organisation beyond campus: they allowed prominent local student activists to liaise with one another on a scale above the very local (that of the campus or the township) and acted as an important mechanism for publicising SASO to new groups and members. The schools were run by local activists and frequently attended by national leaders to ensure that SASO ideology was taught as widely and cohesively as possible. In order to increase its reach and impact, SASO also began to publish and disseminate a monthly newsletter in 1970. In this, organisational leaders wrote topical articles about current projects and publicised campus news reports.

Campus and national leaders corresponded regularly by letter and telegram, and travelled and convened the local and regional formation schools, which acted as workshops to inform and prepare SASO members for activism. This frequent correspondence and a few highly mobile individuals (including a role of travelling general secretary) allowed SASO to be responsive quickly on a national scale to issues that arose on local campuses, and this capacity became very important during the early 1970s, as I will argue in the second part of this chapter. The leadership also convened several times a year for National Executive Council meetings, and annually for a General Students Council meeting that included delegates from all active SASO chapters. In order to create even broader solidarity among members, SASO also held annual Intervarsity days during the winter holidays.

In its early years, then, SASO effectively established networks of student activists throughout South Africa, and it built an especially strong branch at Turfloop. It was able to do so largely thanks to the university administration's initially ambivalent response to its founding: SASO's ostensible adherence to many of the university's own founding principles of separation earned it some room to operate at Turfloop in the very early 1970s. However, as it became evident that SASO's politics were quite radical, and as its leaders began to articulate an ideology of Black Consciousness that drew heavily on the writings of men like Frantz Fanon, Stokely Carmichael, and the American Black Power movement, rather than on the separatism of apartheid, the new organisation increasingly gave the administration cause for concern.

## Student protests at Turfloop, 1970–1972

Perhaps most importantly, the Turfloop SRC itself was a bastion of SASO politics. In the period 1970–71 it was led by Onkgopotse Abram Tiro, a SASO activist and later a member of the SASO national executive. Under Tiro's administration the SRC led the Turfloop student body in protest when the university declared its academic autonomy from the University of South Africa (UNISA). UNISA had been responsible for setting the curriculum and granting degrees at Turfloop since its founding in 1959. In January of 1970, that link was severed as Turfloop ceased to be the University College of the North and became the University of the North.

This change of name and ostensible autonomy changed relatively little in the governing structure of Turfloop; though UNISA no longer conferred the degrees of its graduates, the new university was autonomous in name only. The University of the North Act No. 47 of 1969 (section 14) reaffirmed the control of the minister of Bantu Education over appointments to and decisions made by the University Senate and Council, its two governing bodies. In addition, the minister had the power to approve or reject all funding for the university, even that received through donations.[6] The veneer of independence was thin at best. Though the university was not beholden to UNISA any longer, it was still clearly under the jurisdiction of the Department of Bantu Education and subject to the apartheid-style ethnic segregation of its founding.

In September 1970, when invited to take part in celebrations for this independence and the investiture of the university's first chancellor, students boycotted the celebrations in protest. The alleged autonomy, they contended, was a farce, 'another calculated move by the government to drive the non-white students into a life of isolation, despair and perpetual frustration'.[7] Independence from UNISA was considered premature, and designed not to liberate the university but to further isolate it from its peers in South Africa. To this end, the SRC resolved that:

> if independence has to be true to its meaning, such independence should
> also relate not only to academic independence of this College [but also to
> independence] from Government control, because we hold the following
> to be true ... University autonomy means and implies 'the right of a
> university to decide for itself, on academic grounds, who shall teach,
> and what shall be taught, and who shall be admitted to study'. And these
> conditions can certainly not hold in terms of Act No. 47 of 1969.[8]

These boycotts indicate the increasing activism that was brewing on campus as the ties between the SRC and SASO grew. In 1972 the SRC presidency was taken over by Tiro's deputy, Aubrey Mokoena. Their outspoken politics were to bring the tensions that had been brewing between SASO, the SRC, and the administration, to a head in the autumn of 1972.

On 29 April 1972, the University of the North graduated its third class as an "autonomous" university, and Onkgopotse Tiro spoke as the elected speaker for the graduating class. Tiro had been a prominent student leader on campus since his arrival in the late 1960s, and was a member of the SRC and of SASO. He was president of the SRC that led the boycotts of the celebrations of university autonomy. At the time of his selection as speaker he had completed his bachelors degree in Education, and was working towards his post-graduate diploma in Education.[9] By this time Tiro was already very politically engaged. His activism had early roots: he had been exposed to political protest at the age of twelve, when, in 1957, his local primary school in the village of

Dinokana, near the Botswana border, was closed as thousands of local women protested the introduction of pass laws. This led to a frequently interrupted education in a series of schools in the western Transvaal and Soweto. By the time he completed matric at Barolong High School in Mafikeng, he was already a student leader, and was elected to speak at the leavers' party. According to Barolong Principal Lekalake, 'Tiro's speech about the conditions the pupils were subjected to was so influential that dramatic changes were made immediately in the make-up of the school's administration'.[10] This gift for transformative oratory was to become his hallmark at Turfloop and beyond.

Tiro's invitation to speak at the 1972 graduation was issued by the sitting Student Representative Council. His speech was a damning oration of Bantu Education and the broader discriminatory policies of apartheid, particularly its manifestations at Turfloop. Tiro's speech married the structural injustices of Bantu Education, and apartheid itself, with the local realities faced by students at Turfloop, and it was laced with the hypocrisy he saw there. He criticised apartheid on its own terms, beginning with a quote from South African Prime Minister John Vorster: 'Addressing an ASB [Afrikaanse Studente Bond] congress in June last year Mr Vorster said "[n]o black man has landed in trouble for fighting for what is legally his". Although I don't know how far true this is, I make this statement my launch pad'.[11] Tiro went on to critique the failures of apartheid in its manifestation at Turfloop: the fact that an ostensibly black university was run by white administrators and staffed predominantly by white faculty; that, absurdly, its bookshop was only open to whites; that it awarded university contracts to a white administrator rather than a local black supplier; and that vacation jobs on campus were allocated to white students 'when there are [Turfloop] students who could not get their results due to outstanding fees'.[12] He decried the indignities that parents of the graduates were forced to undergo, being kept outside the hall while white dignitaries sat in the front rows. He called for a black university to have black leadership, and to allocate jobs and contracts for its functioning within the black community. 'The system is failing,' Tiro declared. 'It is failing because even those who recommended it strongly, as the only solution to racial problems in South Africa, fail to adhere to the letter and spirit of the policy'.[13] He closed on a ringing note of warning to university and apartheid authorities, saying:

[i]n conclusion Mr Chancellor I say: [l]et the Lord be praised, for the day

shall come when all men shall be free to breathe the air of freedom and when that day shall come, no man, no matter how many tanks he has, will reverse the course of events. God bless you all![14]

The aftermath of this speech was in some ways predictable, and in others extraordinary. Appalled at the perceived abuse of the platform he had been given, the rector and Advisory Council of the University of the North expelled Tiro. The University Senate, all members of which were white, concurred. In response, following a mixed meeting of both black and white staff, the black academic staff of the university walked out in protest, students at Turfloop boycotted lectures, and the national committee of SASO began to mobilise. Tiro's expulsion set off protests of solidarity, not only at Turfloop, but also elsewhere around South Africa at other black universities and colleges. Though the University of the North authorities insisted that Tiro was the only culprit to be blamed, this was a clear miscalculation. They failed to realise that his words had had an electrifying and galvanising effect. Percy Mokwele, a young black lecturer in Education who was present recalled, '[w]hen Tiro addressed the graduation ceremony we were there in the hall. And during his talk students cheered, cheered and accepted what he was saying. And some black members of staff – especially the younger ones – also cheered'.[15]

## Conclusion

Aggressive action marked the general approach of the University of the North administration to Tiro's speech, and it was to become a hallmark of the relationship between the university and its students throughout the 1970s and 1980s. The administration banned SASO from campus in the aftermath of the "Tiro incident". In reaction to Tiro's expulsion, students organised a boycott of lectures in protest until Tiro was either readmitted or tried by tribunal.[16] In response to this, the university administration summarily expelled *all* students from Turfloop and required each to apply for readmission. This heavy-handed tactic allowed administrators to pick and choose whom to readmit, with some knowledge of which student leaders played especially influential and political roles. In the end, the entire SRC and some other influential student leaders were denied readmission for a period of at least two years.

Banning SASO on campus proved ineffective, though. After the expulsion of Tiro and so many other student leaders in 1972, other students were willing and able to step into their shoes. Where once anti-apartheid politics had been the province of a radical minority, now, according to student leaders from disparate groups, the majority of the student body supported them.[17] Thanks to SASO's bulk-affiliation method through the SRC, and to its frequent and widespread meetings and formation schools, most members were conscientised to the political situation. But another significant factor in the mobilisation of students lay at the feet of the university administration itself: their strict punishment of Tiro, and the extreme reaction of expelling all students, served to galvanise not just the students and staff of Turfloop, but also their fellows at black universities across the country. Boycotts and protests on campus became frequent, almost routine. In the winter of 1972 students at Turfloop were out of lectures almost as much as they were in.

It is worth noting that the depth of conscientisation varied. Not all students became core SASO activists, and many (though by no means all) left their activism behind after university and went into administrative jobs sometimes in the very structures against which they had protested. But in the context of the very local and specific concerns of life at Turfloop – the overreach of the university authorities, and the effective mobilisation by groups on campus like SASO and the SRC – students protested in huge numbers with stay aways, boycotts, and walkouts.

The impact of these protests was felt well beyond Turfloop's walls. Just months after his expulsion Tiro moved to Soweto where he secured a job teaching History at Morris Isaacson High School. Teaching became an outlet for many politically active university students who were expelled in waves of protest at places like Turfloop between 1972 and 1974. In his testimony after the Soweto Uprising of 1976, Aubrey Mokoena, the former Turfloop student and president of the SRC who had arranged Tiro's speech, noted that '[the Black People's Convention] and SASO had some of its members teaching in schools … It was the duty of these people to conscientise students with regard to the struggle for liberation'.[18] Among these teachers, Mokoena noted Tiro at Morris Isaacson, himself at Orlando North Secondary, Tom Manthata at Sekano Ntoane High School, and Cyril Ramaphosa and Lybon Mabasa at Meadowlands High School. All of these except Manthata had been students at Turfloop and were expelled for their political activities, and all of these schools went on to play significant roles in the 1976 uprising.

In addition, the alumni of Turfloop from the early 1970s played roles in a wide range of political activities and groupings over the following decades. Like those mentioned in Mokoena's testimony, Frank Chikane also spent time as a teacher – as a Maths tutor and an informal political teacher to students at his old high school, Naledi High in Soweto. He then went on to become a minister and eventually came to head the South African Council of Churches during the 1980s, which was a vocal critic of the National Party government. Pandelani Nefolovhodwe, who briefly simultaneously held the position of SASO national president and president of the Turfloop SRC in 1974, went to teach Science in the Venda homeland capital of Sibasa. He made sure to reserve some lesson time each week to discuss current political affairs.[19] After his own stint as a teacher in Soweto, Cyril Ramaphosa became a labour organiser, and the first secretary general of the National Union of Mineworkers (NUM) in 1982. NUM became a powerful force in mobilising workers, especially under the banner of the Congress of South African Trade Unions (COSATU) after its formation in 1985, and Ramaphosa rose through the ranks of the United Democratic Front and later the ANC. Meanwhile, Ramaphosa's Turfloop classmates and comrades in the Student Christian Movement there, Ishmael Mkhabela and Lybon Mabasa, launched the Azanian People's Organisation (AZAPO) after the banning of Black Consciousness (BC) organisations in the late 1970s. AZAPO became the primary torch-bearer for BC into the 1980s and 90s.

A particular confluence of circumstances and actors made all these impacts possible. Turfloop's situation as an apartheid/homeland university provided fertile ground and particular forms of daily oppression around which students organised. The South African Students' Organisation gave them the structures and networks through which to do so. These factors combined to project Turfloop's political influence far beyond the isolation of its origins in the rural northern Transvaal, and fostered its growth as a regional and national centre for student activism.

## Endnotes

1   This chapter draws on material from my unpublished DPhil thesis, A History of Youth Politics in Limpopo, 1967–2003, Oxon, 2014.

2   A. Heffernan, A History of Youth Politics in Limpopo, 1967– 2003, unpublished DPhil thesis, University of Oxford, 2014, 31.

3    Interview with Harry Nengwekhulu by Anne Heffernan, Pretoria, 19 October 2011.

4    JGE. Wolfson, *Turmoil at Turfloop: A Summary of the reports of the Snyman and Jackson Commissions of Inquiry into the University of the North*. Johannesburg: SA Institute of Race Relations, 1976, 12.

5    SASO meeting minutes, c. 1969–1976. [WHP (Wits Historical Papers) AD1126/J, A2176/4].

6    Quoted in C. White, *From Despair to Hope: The Turfloop Experience*. Sovenga: University of the North Press, 1997, 122.

7    Telegram to the President of the UCM from AR. Tiro, President of the SRC of the University of the North, 30 September 1970, Sovenga. [WHP AD1126/F].

8    Telegram to the President of the UCM from AR. Tiro, President of the SRC of the University of the North, 30 September 1970, Sovenga. [WHP AD1126/F].

9    Interview with Pandelani Nefolovhodwe by Anne Heffernan, Germiston, 27 September 2011.

10   A. Heffernan, Black Consciousness' Lost Leader: Abraham Tiro, the University of the North, and the Seeds of South Africa's Student Movement in the 1970s, *Journal of Southern African Studies,* 2015, Vol. 41(1), 173-186.

11   South African History Online (SAHO): http://www.sahistory.org.za/archive/graduation-speech-onkgopotse-tiro-university-north-29-april-1972.

12   GM. Nkondo, *Turfloop Testimony: The dilemma of a black university in South Africa*, Johannesburg: Ravan Press, 1976, 91.

13   Nkondo, 1976, 92.

14   Nkondo, 1976, 93.

15   Interview with Percy Mokwele by Anne Heffernan, Turfloop, 20 September 2011.

16   SASO Memo from Rubin Phillip, 24 May 1972. [WHP A2176/3].

17   Interview with Pandelani Nefolovhodwe by Anne Heffernan; Interview with Sydney Seolanyanne by Anne Heffernan, Parktown, Johannesburg, 24 November 2011.

18   Deposition of Aubrey Mokoena taken by Justice of the Peace DL. Aspelling in Johannesburg. Undated (c. early 1977). [WHP A2953].

19   Interview with Pandelani Nefolovhodwe by Anne Heffernan, Germiston, 27 September 2011.

Anne Heffernan is a post-doctoral researcher in the History Workshop at the University of the Witwatersrand with particular interest in the history of political activism among students and youth in South Africa, and the role of educational institutions in anti-apartheid protest. Her research focuses predominantly on Limpopo Province, and she is interested in the ways that ideas move through and across communities, particularly via urban and rural linkages.

# CHAPTER 6

# ACTION AND FIRE IN SOWETO, JUNE 1976[1]

SIBONGILE MKHABELA

I n the 1960s and 70s Naledi High School was the pride of the sprawling, poor, western-most townships of Soweto. This was a school of students who saw themselves as people who would one day play a key role in uplifting black people. Mr Rudolph Mthimkhulu, the founding principal of Naledi, had instilled in them a sense of purpose, ambition, drive, self-love, and a vision of the possible. His belief in the capability of all children, irrespective of their socio-economic background, was infectious. Mr Mthimkhulu was not going to let any one of us feel comfortable about making excuses for Bantu Education. He insisted that it was precisely because of Bantu Education that we needed to prove ourselves and demonstrate to all that we could do it.

My dream as a young kid at Zola Primary School had been to proceed to Naledi High School, which was in a neighbouring township five minutes' walk from home. Instead, after finishing primary school, we were marched to a new school named after Dr BW Vilakazi. I hated the school and it was far away, about an hour's walk from home. We suspected that the reason we were marched to Dr Vilakazi was a continuation of the infamous government policy of 'divide and rule'. Naledi High School was in Naledi township, a predominantly Sotho community, while Dr Vilakazi High School was in a Nguni township – the government discouraged any mixing of the ethnic groups.

When the Department of Bantu Education first had the ridiculous notion of teaching black children through the medium of Afrikaans in 1974, Mr Gqibithole, the principal at Dr Vilakazi, was among the first to agree to implement and test the policy. That first year we all tried very hard to learn. We struggled together with our teachers, who ended up teaching in English and examining pupils' performance in Afrikaans. Heaven knows how they managed to mark the examination scripts! Many of us failed that year, and we did everything we could to transfer to Naledi High School. This was difficult, because Naledi prided itself on academic excellence and could not take a group of failed students.

All was not lost, however. The Young Women's Christian Association (YWCA) facilitated a positive reawakening among young people, and with its strong female leadership, it was like home to me. My mother had died in 1971, but as I interacted with MaKhuzwayo, MaKraai, MaMadlala, and other powerful women, they seemed to be Ma reincarnated. They invited us to the Dube Library for readings, political discussions, and other youth activities. It was exciting to listen to people such as Dr Ellen Khuzwayo, Bro Tom Manthata, George Wauchope, and others. South African Students' Organisation (SASO) leaders were organising students through the work of institutions such as the YWCA and convening seminars which addressed the political and social issues of the day. As a result of these seminars, young minds began to shift more and more towards a critical awareness promoted by, and linked to, the philosophy of Black Consciousness.

The day that I was finally admitted to Naledi High School, I celebrated. I had worked hard to improve my academic results even with Afrikaans as a medium of instruction. After the June examinations I had applied to be admitted at Naledi, and in December I received a letter notifying me that I was conditionally accepted pending my year-end examination results. I was thrilled. I declared myself a Naledi pupil from the moment I received that letter. It was the end of 1974.

## The days before 16 June

On 8 June 1976 Naledi High School was forced to take a stand. I remember that it began as another ordinary school day. We had just come back to class after our routine un-nourishing lunch. The class was as boisterous as ever. Everything was ordinary, very ordinary. Our teacher was beginning his lesson when the principal, JOK Tsotetsi (who had been Mr Mthimkhulu's deputy), suddenly walked in and without apology asked for Enos Ngutshana. Enos was my friend and my comrade in a number of student groups. He was the president of the Student Christian Movement (SCM) at Naledi, and a member of the South African Students' Movement (SASM), of which I was the general secretary in 1976. That afternoon we sensed that something was about to happen. It was not common for the principal to walk into a classroom during lessons or to call students out of classes. We raised our voices and spontaneously interrogated the principal as to why he wanted to talk to Enos outside the classroom.

At that moment the normal situation turned into a tense one. We had earlier noticed a strange white car that was parked outside, next to the principal's office. Police and strangers who arrived in white cars were certainly not our usual visitors or friends. The "system" was represented by everything associated with the Department of Bantu Education through to the hated policemen on the ground. It is important and noteworthy that community schools, administrators, teachers, and pupils were all standing together against the system.[2]

The principal stood at the door that day, not saying much. He said enough in his silence, however, to make us understand that we should expect serious trouble from the system. Enos moved forward, accompanied by the principal. The mood in the class and the whole school changed. We feared for his safety and our own and real anger prevailed. Silence followed Enos' exit. Our classroom was a few metres away from the school principal's office, and we watched them through the windows as they walked into the office. Naledi High School felt personally and grossly invaded.

In the silence, confusion, fear, and anger of the moment, the police car outside the principal's office suddenly burst into flames. Enos escaped unhurt. The two policemen, with fear in their eyes, quickly locked themselves in the principal's office and waited for reinforcements. These came fast and furious. In no time, members of the police and the defence force had completely surrounded the school. The panic on the side of the system was extreme and spectacular. The two cowards had obviously expected to simply walk into the school, arrest a pupil, and that would be that. Their naiveté was something to marvel at.

When working people returned to their homes that evening they found the township in a state of pandemonium and buzzing about the Naledi High School incident. The police had, as usual, overreacted in their response. Sirens, tear gas, and general aggression took over from the shebeens' drunken noises that night. Excited young people milled on the streets.

That night when my father, Baba, came home, he did not say a word. I was authoritatively summoned to his bedroom. A summons from Baba was something none of us looked forward to. When I walked in that day, I knew he was mad but I was also puzzled. He offered me a chair (not a good sign). He continued staring at the ceiling as he spoke. At that moment all my "street wisdom" was gone. He was not asking me to tell him who did what, he was asking searching questions about the school. When Baba wanted an explanation, he received it. But this day I had no explanation. Not getting much joy out of me, I saw Baba toss and turn on his bed in grave distress. He was not going to scold me. He was not angry, but scared. He was worried. For the first time in my life Baba gave me a full political lecture. He talked, almost to himself, about the brutality of white people and the failed struggles of black people. For a brief moment he talked about something he never, ever talked about: his people and country of origin, Mozambique.

I left Baba's room in deep reflection and inner conflict. I wanted to ask him some disturbing questions, but I had lost the pluck and opportunity, because Baba had gone back into his shell and could not be drawn out further. I wanted to ask him what he thought we should do. I wanted to tell him that, as much as I was afraid, I knew what needed to be done. I was certain that change would come only if we committed ourselves as individuals. I knew I had reached a point of no return. The pain was intense and deep. Our lives as black people were in sharp contrast to what was promised in the Christian Bible. My political conviction had become part of my being, and portions of scripture such as 'I am the father of the oppressed', 'I clothe the poor and feed the hungry', and 'All men are created in the image of God', haunted me. These had to be true, and as a Christian, I strongly believed that I had a unique role to play promoting the dignity of all.

In the chaos of the day, Enos Ngutshana had escaped, but the system soon caught up with him. He was arrested a few days after the 8 June incident.

## Action and fire

The simmering tension in the schools in early June 1976 would have alerted anyone to the danger inherent in the spirit of rebellion among the students. We needed an outlet for our pent-up energy. The junior secondary school students were already mobilising themselves against Afrikaans as a medium of instruction. They were taking the campaign to the streets. It was clear to us that our obligation was on the side of our younger sisters and brothers. Afrikaans meant further subjugation, and it was another way of ensuring that black children had very few chances in life. On Friday, 11 June, SASM finally acted. We convened an extraordinary student body meeting after school, instead of holding the usual SASM meeting. We discussed the crisis at black schools, police brutality, and the calculated plan to put pupils in detention. We, the leadership, then invited students to the next meeting, which SASM was planning to convene to discuss these issues with the entire student body of Soweto. The meeting was to be held at the Donaldson Community Centre (DOCC) in Orlando East, on Sunday, 13 June.

DOCC was a huge community hall, and the pride of the people of Soweto. It sat comfortably in the old Orlando township which was known for its pioneering civil rights actions led by the late Mr Sofasonke Mpanza. Approaching DOCC that day I could see groups beginning to converge on the venue from various directions. The students were obviously excited, gesturing animatedly. There was a sense of urgency and seriousness.

Tempers flared high at the meeting, for we all felt it was time we took action. The government's continued insistence on imposing Afrikaans as a medium of instruction on junior secondary schools had undermined the education of the children and had to be stopped. Pupils shared stories about cruel police activities in their schools. We all understood that while the imposition of Afrikaans was a catalyst for action, it was not the real issue. The real issue was to free ourselves from an education that aimed to keep us as "boys" and "girls". The imposition of Afrikaans was an opportunity given to us by the system to stand up and say once and for all that "it is enough". Someone had to fight the system by all means possible. The price to be paid would be less damaging than the passive acceptance of the status quo. This was a fight for "Education", our right to education and what our parents had always valued as the only way to free ourselves.

I made my sentiments clear at the meeting, which, I think, is the reason I ended up being elected onto the Action Committee, which became the Student Representative Council (SRC) that was tasked with the responsibility of organising protest meetings and actions. The students agreed that 16 June was the day when all the students of Soweto would march in protest against Afrikaans, Bantu Education, and the illegitimate South African government. The list of students' grievances grew longer every day. I was happy to be finally involved in direct social action. For too long I had been part of discussions about the government (since I was a small child) and now, in my final months as a teenager, I had a chance to make a meaningful contribution.

The events of the cold morning of 16 June 1976 are written in blood, ash, and tears. I met with other student leaders to review plans before the march, which was scheduled to begin at 06h30. The direction the march was to follow was clear. Those coming from the west would meet with other students at central designated points. The Naledi group would proceed northwards via Zola, Emdeni, Jabulani, Zondi, Mofolo North, Mofolo Central, Dube, and Orlando West townships, and finally all schoolchildren would meet at the Orlando Stadium where the student representatives would lead discussions about Afrikaans and the Department of Bantu Education, and draw up a petition for the Department. After this act of solidarity the students would disperse. It sounded terribly simple, too simple. To ensure that the march was disciplined, and that all the students were accounted for at all times, we agreed to march in rows, each row consisting of five students, holding hands. Each student was responsible for the person whose hand he or she held. From afar the students looked like cornrows.

There was something beautiful and dignified about the gathering of the students that morning at Naledi High School. The girls were in black-and-white check tunics and the boys wore grey pants, white shirts, and black blazers. As we left the school gates we chanted the sorrowful *Senzeni na? Isono sethu bubumnyama lamabhunu ayizinja* (What have we done? Our crime is our blackness. These white rulers are dogs). As we led the big march our spirits lifted and the songs began to be more spontaneous and full of vitality. *Sizobadubula ngembhay'mbhayi,* a song by Miriam Makeba, was among the most popular freedom songs on that morning, but we also made up songs as we marched, converting religious hymns and choruses to freedom songs.

The first tear gas canister landed unexpectedly between my sister Sindile and me. This threw the entire march into chaos. At that point we were approaching Mofolo North. We broke ranks and ran to nearby houses to get help and water to soak our faces and douse the smoke. We carried water in whatever containers we could find and soaked our school tunics with it. Students who collapsed were pulled into nearby homes. Soweto residents opened their hearts and homes to us, in a manner we had never experienced before.

The students who were monitoring the march made an announcement on the loud hailer that took us all by complete surprise: 'A little primary schoolboy has been shot dead in Orlando West, please proceed with great care'. 'Amandla! Viva! Long live!'. The shockwaves went rippling through the masses of marching students resulting in more anger, fear, and chaos. The small boy who died, Hector Pieterson, would later be known throughout the world. My heart pounded hard as tears welled in my eyes. How is it possible that a young, fragile, innocent life could be lost? I was part of the planning. I knew how careful we had tried to be. Why did the little boy die?

We regrouped and quickened our pace. We still believed we would reach Orlando Stadium. We were soon in Orlando West. The air was now more foul. Gunshots could be heard. Students retaliated and threw stones at passing police cars. This is where the protesters earned the name of "stone throwers". What is a stone compared to a gun, any gun, let alone an army rifle?

The next thing we knew a young woman was wriggling in pain on the ground in front of us. She was badly shot in the thigh. Boys picked her up and rushed with her to a nearby house. The crowd at this stage was in total panic and disarray. The members of the South African Defence Force had been brought in to defend South Africa against its own unarmed children! They were shooting to kill, aiming at any figure in grey pants or females in school tunics.

What happened on that fateful day and in the following weeks, months, if not years, has been partially documented as a piece of the history of our struggle. Suffice to say that the march never ended; it took on a life of its own. It created its own heroes and villains, new friends and enemies were born or murdered, another Sharpeville was replayed in our enslaved land. The system had unilaterally escalated its hostility and aggression against the community to an ugly level. We probably needed this push to help us intensify and re-orient our mobilising. The student body became better organised as the Soweto Students' Representative Council (SSRC) was formally established and given a fresh, unambiguous mandate. David Kutumela and I became the official representatives of Naledi High School in the SSRC. SASM also enjoyed much more support from the students. The entire Soweto community stood up in support of the struggle.

## After 16 June

In August 1976, the system caught up with me, and I was arrested. I had spent weeks planning the worker and student stay away that would take place on 24 August. We had taken the struggle to a different level, by appealing to our working and toiling masses to join students in an assault on the system. The strategy adopted by the SSRC involved talking to kids and asking them to appeal to their parents not to go to work on the day. "Azikwelwa!", which is a call for a work stay away, was our rallying battle cry. The strategy behind the plans of 24 August 1976 was to achieve more than only a march. The townships were supposed to stay quiet, with no movements of workers on the way to work. This was the day to hit the white economy.

On 23 August I slept in Sis Thoko's room. Thoko, my eldest sister, lived with her husband Zodwa Mbusi in a backyard room at Emdeni. I remember the sounds of rude, heavy knocks that woke me up. I shudder as I recall the fear that gripped me that morning when armed men kicked at the doors. The door was suddenly kicked open and I heard some chaotic noises outside. I knew the game was up. They were two black men, one very tall and looking particularly happy with his catch. I remember thinking, 'Arresting a young fellow black would probably earn you your promotion. This is what you might have been looking forward to in order to win the favour of your white masters'.

I was then firmly grabbed by the collar of my nightdress and thrown against the door. I felt like a rag doll, but I was determined to maintain some dignity in all of this. As I lifted my face, one of them slapped or punched me and blood spurted out of my mouth. I could hear my sister sobbing in the background. I wished to die. In fact, I remember how in the days that followed I would try to bargain with God for a painless death.

In my skimpy blood-stained nightdress I was driven to the Protea police station in the south of Soweto. The morning was beautiful and I felt the moderately chilly August breeze. From the police car I was practically shoved into a stuffy, windowless cell. The day to come was long and painful. The 14-hour interrogation consisted of being kicked and slapped around by six well-built white policemen. I felt so tired, numb, and listless, and only wanted a place to lay my head and rest.

Eventually I was moved to the central Johannesburg police station known as John

Vorster Square. The cell was huge. So big was the room that it looked as if two Zola houses like my family's would fit in it quite comfortably. The first things I noticed were the windows. The only windows were small, totally covered by mesh, and they were near the very high ceiling. It felt spooky. This was to be my cage for the next three months. I was detained under the notorious Section 6 of the Terrorism Act of 1967, which gave the state the power to detain anybody indefinitely without trial.

During the first days of my confinement this room was completely dark and horribly cold. I learnt to survive, however. One of the things I learnt was that if I climbed on the toilet seat and held onto the wall like a fly I could reach the bars of the window and hold onto them. This became my favourite spot and my link with the world outside. I could see blue skies and people walking on the street below. One day in warm September I saw from my window someone I thought I recognised and I looked more closely. It was my brother Saul! I instinctively screamed out 'Bhuti!' He heard and recognised my voice. I kept on calling so that he could see where I was. We were both overwhelmed and cried.

This became a secret ritual. Saul came to that spot almost daily for the duration of my detention at the notorious John Vorster Square. Others joined him and this became the visitors' spot. Often the visitors had to scan the environment outside, as the police were becoming curious about all these people regularly gathering outside.

I was released from detention in December 1976. In January 1977 the government set a new date for the writing of the aborted 1976 examinations. The date was March 1977. Student leaders were not in agreement about what should be done. A meeting at Naledi High School to resolve the issue only threw the student body into an intense and fiery debate. Tempers flared among the contending factions. The SSRC finally reached a compromise, and the least polarised and confrontational decision was made: we could not force anyone to write or not to write. My closest friends and I also debated among ourselves on this issue. We agreed to differ. I decided not to sit for examination. My personal decision not to write was based totally on principle, strengthened by what I had gone through in prison, and by how I had internalised and taken a position on the issues of the day. Although I felt like this, with every fibre of my being I yearned for a good education. My exposure to Black Consciousness had further turned my thinking to the importance of education and the need to be better prepared for life to handle the white oppressors. Publically I had something to demonstrate, and that was my ability to stand tall and firm in the midst of adversity.

Nearly a year after the events of June 1976, I and ten other leaders of the SSRC were arrested and tried for sedition in May 1977. I was the only female defendant among the "Soweto 11", and was convicted and sentenced to six years in prison (with four deferred). After being shifted to women's jails around the country, I was released from the Johannesburg Fort in May 1982. As I walked through the gate that day I raised my right hand in a power salute: "Amandla!" The response was deafening, "AWETHU!" I was home again. I was home.

## Endnotes

1  This chapter is drawn from excerpts from Mkhabela's autobiography, *Open Earth and Black Roses: Remembering 16 June 1976*. Johannesburg: Skotaville, 2001.

2  The "system" is a representation of the apartheid regime and all its representatives and aligned institutions such as the Department of Bantu Education.

Sibongile Mkhabela is the chief executive officer of the Nelson Mandela Children's Fund. She also serves as an independent non-executive director of Barloworld Limited, and was a consultant programme officer for the United Nations Development Programme. As a teenager, she was one of the leaders of the 1976 Soweto Uprising.

# CHAPTER 7

# WHAT *THEY* SHOT IN ALEX

S T E V E   K W E N A   M O K W E N A

J une 16, 1976 is one of the most photographed moments in South African history. When the photojournalist Sam Nzima took the picture of 13-year-old Hector Pieterson dying in the arms of Mbuyisa Makhubu, he could not have known that, with that click of the camera, he would be marking a historical turning point. This picture has travelled all over the world and has become the iconic image of the June 16, 1976 student revolt. The picture said it all, so to speak. But this is not the only visual story to be told.

This photographic essay is made up of moments captured by the police photographers and embedded reporters. The essay revisits June 16, 1976 through their lenses. It looks at what they saw and what they shot. The essay is made up of 16 images from Alexandra Township in Johannesburg. The police photographer pointing his camera at the children, just like the policeman pointing a gun, is a missing voice in the historiography of the June 16 student revolt. These unnamed photographers came with the police to document the "riots". The photographers' lenses were there to pick up evidence of "rioting" and destruction. The photographs used in this essay were compiled as part of the Cillie Commission, which was tasked to investigate the causes and consequences of the June 16 uprising for the government of the day. Although the photo essay is an open-ended conversation made up of a subjective selection of images, (pictures that moved me) it is also guided by two impulses: first, to show that June 16 started in Soweto but it ignited fires in other parts of the country, thus the focus on Alexandra, and second, because the pictures are shot from the sky, or from behind the police line, they reveal something disturbing about the confrontation between the white riot policeman and the African child, both caught in a fiery historical moment.

Alexandra, street scene, aerial view

Alexandra, truck burning with crowd

Alexandra, police watching
building burn

Alexandra, destroyed bottle store

Alexandra, crowd and police confrontation

Alexandra, crowd with posters,
'Today for us All'

Alexandra, children

Alexandra, crowd with poster,
'Don't Shoot'

Alexandra, crowd with policeman

Alexandra, crowd

Alexandra, policeman addressing
crowd with bullhorn

Alexandra, man with cane
leading crowd towards police

Alexandra, anxious crowd

Alexandra, man being held
by policeman

Alexandra, policemen

Alexandra, street scene

Steve Kwena Mokwena is an artist, filmmaker, cultural activist and curator with deep roots in the youth development field. To date Kwena has made over ten films including the award-winning *A Blues for Tiro* (2007) and *Driving with Fanon* (2009). His latest film *Jazz Heart* (2015) premiered at the Encounters South African International Documentary Festival. As a curator, Kwena has worked on exhibitions in sites that include 'Number 4' Constitution Hill, Walter Sisulu Square of Dedication, Boipatong, Freedom Park and others. Kwena is also the stationmaster of the AFRIKAN FREEDOM STATION, an Afrocentric multi-media gallery in Johannesburg where he paints. He holds degrees from the Universities of the Witwatersrand and Leeds, and was a visiting scholar at the Institute for Social Studies in The Hague.

CHAPTER 8

# SASO AND BLACK CONSCIOUSNESS, AND THE SHIFT TO CONGRESS POLITICS

SALEEM BADAT

I n 1960, demonstrators protesting against pass laws were killed and injured by police at Sharpeville. Soon afterwards, the apartheid government declared a state of emergency. Over 11 000 political activists were detained, and repressive new laws, police raids, arrests, bannings, and torture were used to crush political opposition to apartheid. The African National Congress (ANC) and Pan Africanist Congress (PAC) were banned, and many leaders of the ANC and PAC were arrested and imprisoned, and hundreds fled into exile.

For many white South Africans, the rest of the 1960s were a time of economic boom, political calm, prosperity, and rising living standards. Some blacks took the opportunity to accumulate wealth, power, and privilege through the Bantustans that the apartheid government established as part of its separate development programme. For most blacks, it was a period of great economic exploitation, extensive political and social control, fear, and demoralisation. It was difficult to see how there could be any political challenge to white minority rule. Anti-apartheid organisations faced immediate repression. They also had to overcome black people's fear and demoralisation, which stood in the way of mobilising opposition against apartheid.

## The emergence of the South African Students' Organisation and Black Consciousness

Despite many problems, the South African Students' Organisation (SASO) was formed as an exclusively black university and college student organisation in 1968. It escaped immediate state repression, and developed a following among students at the universities reserved for blacks. Thereafter, the ideology of Black Consciousness (BC) was developed and other BC organisations were formed, resulting in the BC movement.

SASO saw its challenge as the 'assertion, manifestation and development of a sense of awareness politically, socially and economically among the black community'.[1] It emphasised black 'group cohesion and solidarity' as 'important facets of Black Consciousness', the need for 'the totality of involvement of the oppressed people', and for BC 'to be spread to reach all sections of the black community'.[2] SASO began community development, literacy, education, media, culture, and sports projects, which aimed to help black communities to determine and realise their own needs. They were seen as a means to win the trust of people and to educate and mobilise them.[3] Projects instilled the idea of self-reliance, seen as important for achieving freedom, in members and communities.

SASO created a favourable political climate for various organisations to emerge. It maintained relations with them, and tried to link them into a single national movement. Worker organisations, secondary school student organisations, and youth bodies like the National Youth Organisation (NAYO) were formed, and a political organisation, the Black People's Convention (BPC), was launched. In this way, BC ideas were spread beyond university students.

The pre-1977 BC movement was largely the achievement of SASO. The key ideas of BC came from SASO. BC intellectuals largely cut their political teeth within SASO. For much of its short life, SASO stood ideologically, politically, and organisationally at the head of the BC movement. The scholar Sam Nolutshungu wrote that 'at the centre of the movement, giving leadership, was SASO'.[4]

## The importance of SASO and BC

In the political conditions of the 1960s, the launch of SASO and BC organisations was an important step. It ended the silence and despair of the 1960s, rebuilt black oppositional politics, and inspired a new era of black political activism and resistance. Once again, racial and national oppression and apartheid were challenged, and there was organised opposition to apartheid.

SASO was the first national black political higher education student organisation in South Africa. It survived an authoritarian and repressive political order for almost a decade, which was a major achievement. More significantly, SASO forged black students into an organised, independent political force for national liberation in South Africa and turned universities and colleges into sites of struggle.

BC asked whether a commitment to a non-racial society meant that the political struggle had to be fought through non-racial organisations, and contact with white or multi-racial organisations. Were the membership of an organisation and its strategy determined only by principles and goals, or also by social and political conditions? By being exclusively black in membership, BC organisations allowed blacks to stand 'at the touchlines' no longer, and instead to 'do things for themselves and all by themselves'.[5] They provided political education and organisational training, and the 'experience of leadership, planning, strategising and mobilising'.[6] They also provided black students, youth, and other social groups an alternative political home from that of the black political parties involved in separate development institutions.

SASO's support among black students largely stopped the attempt by the apartheid government and business to co-opt students and expand the ruling class. Instead SASO won students over to a radical project of national liberation, which meant seeing their futures as inextricably tied to those of other oppressed people. Using Black Consciousness, SASO led black students in protests and revived organised opposition to apartheid. At secondary schools, SASO educated, mobilised and organised students. The defeat of Portuguese colonialism and success of liberation struggles in Angola and Mozambique gave confidence to black youth and contributed to their militancy. In 1976, when the apartheid government insisted that Afrikaans should be the language of instruction for some school subjects, students in Soweto were ready to take action. The subsequent student protest marches, police shootings, countrywide student boycotts, parent demonstrations, and stay aways became part of the Soweto Uprising of 1976–77, which challenged white minority rule and apartheid power and domination. As in the early 1960s, the apartheid government used police and army terror, shootings, mass arrests, detentions, and banning of individuals to smother black political resistance. Through its contribution to the Soweto Uprising, and the subsequent flow of students and youth into exile, SASO gave to the ANC 'oxygen and new life, which the movement desperately needed – youth of the South African people, tempered in defiance in action'.[7]

The Soweto Uprising was of tremendous political significance. It helped to rebuild political opposition in South Africa, and revitalised the exiled liberation movements. It forced big business to think again about how it could best safeguard its wealth and interests. It forced the apartheid government to introduce various reforms in the hope that through these it could still rule. The uprising produced new and changed conditions of political struggle.

## BC understanding of South Africa and ideology

The BC movement saw race as the main dividing line, and racial and national oppression as the key problem in South Africa. Division in terms of class was not seen as important, and neither for the most part, were gender issues. Whites were collectively identified as "the enemy". Political divisions among whites were interpreted as differences over how best to maintain white privilege and political domination.

The goals and role of white liberals were especially rejected. Biko said that while one sector of whites 'kicked the black', another sector of whites (liberals) 'managed to control the responses of the blacks to the provocation', and tutored blacks 'how best to respond to the kick'.[8] For Biko, it was the black person's 'right and duty to respond to the kick *in the way he sees fit*'.[9] The hold of white liberals over black political thinking had to be broken, by excluding whites from 'all matters relating to the struggle'.[10] Contact with whites was discouraged, and multi-racial organisation was rejected. Despite this, SASO was not anti-white. The exclusive black membership of SASO and BC organisations was a strategy, not a principle. Blacks had to withdraw initially in order to forge black solidarity and unity and formulate their political beliefs and goals. SASO accepted that 'South Africa is a country in which both black and white live and shall continue to live together'.[11] Biko's goal was a 'completely non-racial society [without] guarantees for minority rights', because such guarantees implied 'the recognition of portions of the community on a race basis'. In South Africa there should 'be no minority, just the people. And those people will have the same status before the law and they will have the same political rights'.[12]

Previously black people had been termed "non-white". BC rejected this term and positively identified as "black" all those who are 'by law or tradition politically, economically and socially discriminated against as a group in the South African society'.[13] All Africans, Indians, and coloureds, collectively, were therefore "black". The term "black" was a deliberate attempt by BC to counter the divide and rule strategy of the apartheid government.

## Ideological and political shifts

At first, SASO and the BC movement were ideologically and politically united. South African society was analysed in terms of race, racism, and racial domination. The counter to black oppression was black unity.

After the mid-1970s, differences emerged within the BC movement. Some BC leaders began using the ideas of class, capitalism, and capitalist exploitation to analyse South Africa. In July 1976, the SASO president Diliza Mji argued that the apartheid state was promoting a black middle class, and that this class was already showing that it was eager to join the capitalist system. He said that the black middle class was friendly to 'imperialism, the highest form of capitalism'. Mji argued that the struggle had to be viewed 'not only in terms of colour interests but also in terms of class interests. Apartheid as an exploitative system is part of a bigger whole, capitalism. There are a lot of institutions and practices even amongst ourselves that are part of the general strategy of oppression'.[14]

Mji warned that students could 'be the oppressors of the people if not armed with a clear analysis and strategy, and an accurate perception of who the enemy is and in what forms he is capable of presenting himself'.[15] He said that BC's ability to express 'the aspirations of the masses of the people', depended on 'interpreting our situation from an economic and class point of view'. This would show that the South African struggle was 'part of a bigger struggle of the third world that wants to shake off the yoke of imperialism and replace it with socialistic governments in which power is wielded not by a few wealthy families but by the people'. Mji emphasised developing strong relations with workers, and being 'more organised than before'.[16] One reason for the shift from a race analysis to a race and class analysis of South Africa was that the BC framework did not provide satisfactory answers to the question of black oppressors. The ANC, as well as the South African Communist Party, emphasised the salience of both race and class and their articulation, to give rise in South Africa to a colonialism of a "special type". Another reason was some SASO members were coming into contact with the ANC through its underground members and literature, and Radio Freedom. The strikes of black Natal workers in 1973 showed the power of workers, and suggested that while students were an important part of the anti-apartheid struggle, they were not necessarily the most important grouping.

A BC activist said that they were also learning about 'developments in Mozambique and Angola' and 'from their theories and practices. The ideas of liberation movements like FRELIMO fighting the system of capitalist exploitation and not Portuguese people, as such, and ideas of class struggle filtered through and were giving us light in understanding why blacks like Matanzima were selling out'.[17]

These new ideas were not accepted by all, and 'did not go unchallenged'.[18] There were accusations that SASO 'was turning red' [becoming communist]. Tensions developed between those who supported a race–class analysis and leaned towards socialism, and others who emphasised race and a new society of "black communalism". The idea of black communalism arose at a Black People's Convention (BPC) conference, and was meant to represent a third way 'between capitalism and communism'.[19]

The new line of thinking that appeared in SASO was important because after the Soweto Uprising of 1976–77, there was a struggle within black anti-apartheid politics between this new line of thinking and more traditional BC ideas. The new line of thinking became ideologically and politically dominant in the 1980s. Many of the BC activists who supported a race–class analysis became key cadres of the anti-apartheid movements that supported the ANC in the 1980s.

## Politics after the 1976–77 Soweto Uprising

On 19 October 1977, SASO and various other BC organisations were banned. As a result, anti-apartheid activists everywhere debated the ideology, politics, and strategy and tactics that were most appropriate for the anti-apartheid struggle. This was especially true in prisons, like Modder B in the Transvaal, that held political detainees. According to Mji 'opposing views which had been developing' showed themselves 'within the cells of Modder B'.[20] As a result of differences in analysis, ideology, political orientation, strategy, and tactics, in the years to come there was a major split within anti-apartheid forces between those supporting Black Consciousness, the Azanian Peoples' Organisation (AZAPO), the National Forum, and the Azanian Manifesto, and those who supported the ANC and the Congress movement, the United Democratic Front, and the Freedom Charter.

One of the first national student organisations formed in the late 1970s, the Congress of South African Students (COSAS), supported the Congress movement. So too did the South African Allied Workers Union (SAAWU), which emphasised worker-controlled trade unions, and the leading role of the working class in the national liberation struggle. Local and regional-level community organisations that emerged in various areas and mobilised people around housing, rents, electricity, and transport, were largely led by activists committed to the Congress movement.

During the late 1970s, the divide between the BC and Congress movements was not wide or rigid. Individuals and organisations straddled the political divide. Only later did conflicts around principles and strategies harden, with the first clashes occurring in the student political arena. The Azanian Students' Organisation (AZASO) was formed in 1979 as a BC organisation with close links to AZAPO. However, AZASO soon began to distance itself from AZAPO. Clear evidence of AZASO's shift towards the Congress movement came during the anti-Republic Day protests of early 1981. The student organisations within the anti-Republic Day movement included AZASO, COSAS and, significantly, NUSAS, which in the late 1970s came under a radical leadership that aligned itself with the Congress movement.

AZASO's participation in the anti-Republic Day activities was significant for many reasons. By sharing a platform with NUSAS and white radicals who were linked to black trade unions, AZASO broke with the BC strategy of political struggle on a racially exclusive basis. For the first time in over a decade, national black and white student organisations united in common opposition to apartheid. The joint action with COSAS and NUSAS marked the beginning of a non-racial student alliance committed to the Freedom Charter.

AZAPO criticised AZASO's sharing of platforms with white radicals and there were verbal clashes between the two organisations at a meeting to commemorate the fifth anniversary of the June 1976 uprising. An AZAPO speaker rejected white radicals as liberals, and criticised black students for being 'duped [by their] rhetoric colour-blind, orthodox Marxist language'.[21] AZASO and COSAS described AZAPO members as 'black liberals [who forget that] the struggle continues all the time'. AZAPO was also criticised for having an occasional public profile, and for avoiding day-to-day mobilisation and organisation-building.[22] This clash between AZASO and COSAS and AZAPO showed that the ideological and political differences between the Congress and BC movements were growing.

AZASO's break from BC and commitment to the Congress movement was consolidated at its national congress in late 1981, when an overwhelmingly ANC-supporting leadership was elected. Thereafter, it was in the forefront of promoting a race–class analysis of South Africa, and a non-racial approach to political struggle. In 1985, AZASO changed its name to the South African National Students' Congress (SANSCO), as a way of signalling its commitment to the Congress movement.

Between 1982 and 1985 there were verbal and physical clashes between AZASO members and student supporters of AZAPO at a number of campuses. AZASO blamed the violence on disruptions of its activities by AZAPO supporters, and said that 'ever since AZASO decided to align itself with progressive forces ... AZAPO people have persistently regarded AZASO not just as an opponent but actually as enemy number 1. AZASO has been accused of being Marxist-Leninist, Communist, ANC fronts etc'.[23] Given police repression and the apartheid government's strong hostility to communism and the ANC, it was dangerous to accuse AZASO of being Marxist and an ANC front. Eventually, in 1983, student supporters of AZAPO established the Azanian Students' Movement (AZASM). According to its first president, AZASM was formed when the BC 'faithfuls found themselves politically homeless ... after the up to then BC AZASO abandoned the BC ideology for something "more contemporary"'.[24]

Differences in ideology, politics, and strategy resulted in various other student and youth formations being established, such as the South African Youth Congress, the Azanian Students' Congress, the Pan African Students' Organisation, the Azanian National Youth Unity, and the Students of Young Azania. Each of the student and youth organisations was linked to a parent grouping, such as the Congress movement, the PAC, and the BC movement.

During the period 1982–83, the government introduced constitutional changes that tried to co-opt Indians and coloureds into becoming junior partners in ruling South Africa, while Africans would have political rights only in the Bantustans like Transkei and Venda. In order to oppose and defeat these changes, anti-apartheid organisations created two separate national bodies in 1983. This showed the division among anti-apartheid organisations. One was the Congress movement-supporting United Democratic Front

(UDF), which was made up of over 500 local and regional civic, youth, women's, political, and religious organisations, and national student organisations and trade unions. The other was the smaller National Forum, a loose association of some 200 BC-supporting organisations and small radical groups.

From 1983 onwards the UDF, a popular, non-racial, multi-class alliance, was at the forefront of resistance to apartheid. UDF campaigns resulted in hundreds of new organisations being formed, especially in the rural areas. Tom Lodge, a scholar of the period, writes that the UDF's creation marked a 'shift in the balance of power between the South African government and the black opposition. The UDF inspired an insurrectionary movement that was without precedent in its geographical spread, in its combative militancy, in the burden it imposed on government resources, and in the degree to which it internationalised hostility toward apartheid'.[25] Lodge adds that 'the movement that the UDF headed was profoundly popular, infused "from below" by the beliefs and emotions of "ordinary people". In contrast to earlier phases of black opposition, a class-conscious ideology was the essential motivating force among a large number of its rank and file activists. In this sense, it was a much more radical movement than any that had preceded it'.[26]

The BC movement and other organisations were not irrelevant to the anti-apartheid resistance of the 1980s. However, they were overshadowed by the Congress movement, and their political contribution was of less significance than that of the Congress movement. A writer on youth politics in the mid-1980s wrote that one of the 'most striking characteristics was the overwhelming dominance of the Charterist groupings. Not only in youth structures, but also in the student- and pupil-led organisations, the Congress tradition held sway'.[27]

A very important feature of the 1980s was the development of powerful trade unions among black workers. Low wages and poor working conditions and the work of trade union activists led to hundreds of work stoppages and strikes. Black workers joined unions and built a democratic trade union movement to represent their interests. Some worker strikes gave rise to successful national consumer boycotts of products and had strong support among other organised workers, black students, youth, and township residents. The strikes and the worker-support campaigns created a tradition of worker–student–community action and alliance. In 1985, many anti-apartheid trade unions united to form the half-a-million member strong Congress of South African

Trade Unions (COSATU). COSATU and the UDF were to play a powerful role in ending apartheid rule.

Lastly, the banned ANC was strengthened by people who went into exile during and after the uprising of 1976–77. The ANC began to develop 'a strong clandestine organisation in the country'.[28] ANC members played an important role in shifting activists away from BC and in forming mass organisations. From 1980 onwards, support for the ANC began to be shown openly at mass public meetings, commemoration services, funerals, marches, and demonstrations. ANC leaders in prison and in exile were very popular, and the ANC could claim to have a mass following.

The attacks by the ANC's military wing, Umkhonto we Sizwe (MK), on military facilities and apartheid establishments also built the reputation of the ANC, especially among students and youth. From 13 attacks in 1979, MK attacks increased to 136 in 1985 and 281 in 1989.[29] After 1985, MK tried to root itself more firmly within South Africa, to train and arm local people, and to give leadership to the ANC call to make South Africa "ungovernable".

## Endnotes

1   Black Student Manifesto.

2   SASO Policy Manifesto.

3   R. Fatton, *Black Consciousness in South Africa: The dialectics of ideological resistance to white supremacy*. Albany: State University of New York Press, 1986, 98.

4   SC. Nolutshungu, *Changing South Africa: Political considerations*. Manchester: Manchester University Press, 1982, 149.

5   S. Biko, *Steve Biko: I Write what I Like*. A. Stubbs (ed.). London: Heinemann, 1987, 15.

6   B. Pityana, M. Ramphele, M. Mpumlwana and L. Wilson (eds.). *Bounds of Possibility: The legacy of Steve Biko and Black Consciousness*. Cape Town: David Philip, 1991, 255.

7   Mongane Wally Serote, cited by Pityana et al, *Bounds of Possibility*, 1991, Introduction, 10.

8   Biko, 1987, 66.

9   Biko, 1987, 6, emphasis in original.

10  SASO Policy Manifesto.

11  Ibid.

12  Biko, 1987, 149.

13  SASO Policy Manifesto.

14  SASO Bulletin, 1, 1, 1977.

15 Ibid.

16 Ibid.

17 AZASO National Newsletter, November 1983.

18 Ibid.

19 Ibid.

20 Ibid.

21 Feud Erupts at June 16 Rally, *Cape Times*, 22 June 1981.

22 Ibid.

23 AZASO Official Statement by the National Executive of AZASO on the Incidents at Alan Taylor Residence on 14 May 1983, Saturday, and subsequent events. nd.

24 S. Johnson, The Soldiers of Luthuli: Youth in the politics of resistance in South Africa, in S. Johnson (ed.), *South Africa: No turning back*. Bloomington: Indiana University Press, 1988, 111, quoting an AZASM publication, *Awake Black Student*, March 1985.

25 T. Lodge and B. Nasson (eds.), *All, Here and Now: Black politics in South Africa in the 1980s*. London: Hurst and Company, 1992, 29–30.

26 Ibid.

27 Johnson, 1988, 140-141.

28 Stadler, A. *The political economy of modern South Africa*. Cape Town: New Africa Books, 1987, 160.

29 Lodge and Nasson, 1992, 178.

Saleem Badat is the author of several books on South African students and education. He has served as the director of the Education Policy Unit at the University of the Western Cape, as the first head of the Council on Higher Education, which advises the South African minister of Higher Education and Training, and as vice-chancellor of Rhodes University. He is currently the program director of the International Higher Education and Strategic Projects programme at the Andrew W. Mellon Foundation.

# CHAPTER 9

# YOUTH POLITICS AND RURAL REBELLION IN ZEBEDIELA AND OTHER PARTS OF THE "HOMELAND" OF LEBOWA, 1976–1977[1]

### SEKIBAKIBA PETER LEKGOATHI

The massive eruption of the youth revolt in the township of Soweto near Johannesburg on 16 June 1976 sent shockwaves across the length and breadth of South Africa. Those tremors were felt in many other townships and rural villages almost instantly and in the years that followed until 1994. It was a major turning point as black youngsters took leadership at the forefront of popular resistance against the apartheid state. After 1976, schools, particularly in urban areas on the Witwatersrand, were turned into battlegrounds from which students repeatedly launched offensives against gutter education, authoritarianism and the apartheid system as a whole. While the shockwaves of the 1976 Soweto students' uprising were felt in the countryside, it was only really in the period from the mid-1980s that the urban youth culture of resistance – what Colin Bundy (1987) labelled 'generational consciousness' – became widely entrenched among the rural youth as well.[2] As a result of the social and historical processes that influenced them, rural youth became self-assertive and aware of themselves as a separate social category with a common identity, capable of changing the way their communities operated.

Many books and scholarly articles have been written about youth uprisings in the country but most of these tend to focus on Soweto and other townships on the Witwatersrand, where most of the popular resistance against apartheid was concentrated, with little consideration being given to the countryside. There are two main reasons why very little has been written about the unfolding of the Soweto Uprising in the South African countryside in general, and in the northern parts of the country in particular.

The first reason has to do with researchers' preoccupation with developments in towns, thanks to the relative ease of access to information and shortness of distance to research sites in urban areas. As a result, they have lacked meaningful contact with the countryside or knowledge of issues affecting rural communities. The second reason concerns the forms of struggles and resistance in the countryside that were invariably more low-key and incomplete and not as dramatic or as visible as those unfolding in the urban townships.

This chapter gives a broad overview of the dynamics of youth politics and rebellion in the rural parts of the northern Transvaal – what is known as Limpopo province today – focusing specifically on the rural village of Zebediela, in the 1970s. We will first look at the initial responses to the upheaval in the Polokwane (formerly Pietersburg) area, focusing on the University of the North at Turfloop in Mankweng township, as well as on Pax Institute and Setotolwane Teachers' Training College, both of which are situated near Matlala village on the outskirts of Polokwane. We then take a single school, Matladi Secondary School in the village of Zebediela, as a case study, and explore the unfolding of the unrest in the school in the period 1976–77.

The discussion of youth politics and rebellion at Matladi Secondary School in the mid-1970s is important in the light of continuing scholarly neglect of rural communities. The oldest secondary school in Zebediela, Matladi was built by the local villagers in the 1940s to cater for the educational needs of their children, who needed formal education to secure employment in the growing Bantustan bureaucracy and urban centres. The school is situated at Moletlane, about a stone's throw away from the chief's homestead, approximately 45 kilometres southeast of the town of Mokopane (formerly Potgietersrus). The establishment of boarding facilities at the school in the 1960s, to provide accommodation for students from remote rural villages and urban areas, would bring about some interesting dynamics that affected the manner in which news about the 1976 Soweto students' uprising played out in the area.

By the mid-1970s, a substantial number of students in the school's hostels came from urban townships, particularly from Mamelodi, Atteridgeville and Saulsville in Pretoria, areas that experienced student uprisings in 1976 and 1977. These students were right at the core of student action at the school, and it was largely through them that the news of the revolt in Soweto came to be known at Matladi and other schools in the area.

They were the ones who were best informed about the situation, given their links to family and friends at home. After receiving telegram messages and express letters from parents and guardians informing them about the turmoil, these students went back to the townships to attend funerals. On returning to Matladi, having seen for themselves the situation in the townships on the Rand, and having developed a deeper sense of political consciousness, they wanted all students to embark on a symbolic class boycott in solidarity with the victims of Soweto. However, rural students, who constituted the bulk of day scholars at Matladi, were not keen to be involved in the revolt.

There are two main reasons why the local students did not feel strongly about the need for a class boycott. Firstly, the imposition of Afrikaans as a medium of instruction, used on a par with English, which was one of the main triggers of the uprisings in Soweto and other urban townships, never became a politicising issue at Matladi. The Afrikaans medium policy did not apply in the homelands. In Lebowa, English had already been chosen as a medium of instruction at secondary school level by the early 1970s, but Afrikaans continued to be offered as an additional language. Secondly, there was a complex mixture of urban and rural influences in those schools that muted the formation of a common identity among students and a more forceful articulation of solidarity with the students of Soweto.

## Proliferation of the 1976 student rebellion to the countryside

Let us first look at Turfloop. The students at the University of the North, Turfloop, were among the first to know about the revolt in Soweto. There was a large body of students from urban areas at this institution, which was one of the few universities located in the homeland areas where black students could get higher education. Being one of the most politicised black universities in the country, as well as the bedrock of the Black Consciousness ideology, the University of the North influenced political developments in the schools and teacher training colleges in the region. However, while the influence in the 1980s has been systematically studied, there continues to be a blind spot about the 1970s. It is quite possible that, unlike their urban counterparts, students at Turfloop who came from surrounding rural villages resented class boycotts as they had not yet developed a political culture of militancy and confrontation with the authorities.[3]

The student unrests in Lebowa were not only confined to the University of the North. Pax Institute was one of the schools affected. This boys-only boarding school was established by the Brothers of Charity (Roman Catholic Church) in 1930 in the Mašašane area outside Polokwane. News about the Soweto Uprising arrived at Pax in the evening of 16 June, and the presence of the police and their intimidating approach resulted in some "riotous behaviour" with students breaking the windows of the school.[4] Pax was closed for about three months following this and only reopened in October.[5]

Setotolwane College of Education near the township of Seshego in Polokwane was also touched by the tumult of June 1976. Several buildings of the college, including the library, were set on fire, and as a result the examinations were suspended. This incident occurred after a period of fairly open but heated discussion on whether or not student-teachers should boycott classes in solidarity with the children of Soweto. Coming from an environment where Black Consciousness ideology had made a significant impression on them, students from urban areas were markedly politicised and militant. They questioned why classes at the college should continue as if things were normal when things were clearly not normal and students in Soweto and other townships on the Rand were being killed by the police. They argued in favour of a symbolic class boycott in solidarity with the students of Soweto. Most students from the countryside, however, were not keen, fearing that class boycotts would delay their academic progress and ultimately scupper their chances of employment as teachers.[6] Divisions over the issue of a class boycott at the college very roughly reflected the backgrounds of the students. Disruption of teaching and learning at the college was low-key but continued until late 1977. Actions such as the burning incident alienated and disturbed most of the students, even the urban-based ones who had initially had some sympathy for the boycott. Consequently, the militants never really commanded numerical superiority and in the end the class boycott petered out because of these internal student divisions.[7]

The 1976 Soweto students' uprising also affected many rural boarding schools, including Matladi Secondary School in Zebediela. As argued in the introductory section of this chapter, urban students at Matladi, who were mainly boarders, played a leading role in the upheaval that took place. It was through them that news about the revolt in Soweto came to be known at the school, although access to daily newspapers such as *Bantu World* may also partly have facilitated the dissemination of information about the student revolt among the handful of local students who were curious to know about national developments.[8]

The situation came to a head after the winter vacation when the students returned to school from their various home areas in early July 1976. Some urban students exhorted and cajoled their rural counterparts to join them in a class boycott in solidarity with the children of Soweto. This involved some intimidation and ultimately relations between the two groups soured. The main trigger for the conflict was an assault during break, in September 1976, on a local student by a bullying male boarder with the connivance of several other boarders. The day scholars planned to retaliate by attacking the boarders in their dormitories at night but the large distance between the homes of many local students and the school thwarted such a plan and an attempted daylight assault the following day was easily rebuffed by the boarders. Alfred Matlaila, a student at Matladi during that time, vividly recalls the confrontation:

> When the day scholars were massing outside the school yard, the boarders attacked, holding pillows in their left hands, and the softball bats in their other hands … charging, some with big knives.[9]

The day scholars dispersed in different directions only to regroup later. They started throwing stones at the boarders, using the ample supplies readily available. No major injuries were sustained but the damage to the school property was extensive enough to warrant police investigation. This took place on 23 September.[10] No arrests were made but the atmosphere remained tense and enmity between the two groups persisted in the aftermath of the incident.

Despite the deep-rooted ill feeling between the boarders and day students, there were no other major incidents at the school for over a year. However, in October 1977, another class boycott was called by the boarders 'in protest against Bantu Education'.[11] Most surprisingly, both day scholars and boarders answered the call, which perhaps suggests a steadily growing political consciousness among rural youth in secondary schools in the aftermath of the Soweto students' uprising. The Circuit Inspector of Schools in the District of Mokerong (of which Zebediela formed part) was called by the principal to intervene. He instructed the students to go back home until this explosive situation cooled down.[12] Although the rural students did participate in this protest, it seemed, however, that they did so in a half-hearted manner. Relations between the two groups had been severely damaged by the previous call for a class boycott, and they remained strained until the end of the 1970s.

## Analysing the conflict at Matladi Secondary School

While there was mutual enmity between rural and urban students in boarding schools and tertiary institutions in the rural areas, relations between them were much more complex than is suggested by the somewhat crude urban–rural dichotomy implied above. The situation at Matladi Secondary School serves to illustrate this point. For one thing, not all boarders were from urban areas and not all day scholars were necessarily rural children, though most were. As in other boarding schools in the country, boarders were a mixed group of students from urban townships and rural villages. Some came from rural villages and urban townships around Polokwane, Mokopane, Bochum and from Sekhukhuneland. Boarders were not really a homogenous group sharing a distinctive consciousness, acting against a united group of rural students with a common identity. There were divisions among local students which would be difficult to identify without a thorough exploration of the historical development of education in Zebediela since the 1950s. It is only through a close analysis of these divisions among students that we can arrive at a more nuanced understanding of the upheavals at Zebediela and other institutions in the region in 1976 and 1977.

Briefly, Western-style schooling in African communities in the northern regions of South Africa was introduced, mainly by Christian missionaries, in the late nineteenth and early twentieth centuries. One of the major effects of the presence of missionaries in the area was the physical separation of African communities into believers and non-believers, or Christians and non-Christians. Having embraced the new belief system, Christian converts often denounced "traditional" practices (which they now associated with heathenism) and embraced modern schooling. The "traditionalists", on their part remained hostile to Christianity and clung tenaciously to traditional institutions, chief among which was initiation (*koma* in North Sotho or Sepedi). As a form of youth socialisation, *koma* helped reinforce the authority of chiefs, or traditional leaders and male elders. However, as rural Africans lost their land and their livelihoods as a result of government policies that deliberately sought to turn the people into a pool of cheap labour, the nature of their economy also changed and they had to make the most of what was available for future generations. It is within this context that schooling became very important for both Christians and non-Christians alike.

In his analysis of the situation in Sekhukhuneland, Delius shows that as the nature of the rural economy changed, schooling increasingly became the focal point of, and education a dominant value in, the lives of Christian and non-Christian alike.[13] This happened in Zebediela as well. The increase in the perceived value of schooling had some crucial implications for relations between traditionalist and Christian youth. Within the school setup, these young people found themselves under the same roof, and as a result, the earlier pattern of open hostility gave way to limited fraternisation between traditionalist and Christian youth. Cooperation was reinforced by activities such as the sport (mainly soccer, netball and athletics) that took place in the schools.

As more and more schools were established, formal schooling gradually replaced *koma* as a major form of socialisation outside the household even among non-Christian youngsters. The school calendar came to dictate the duration of the *koma* practice and in many communities it only took place for about a month during the mid-year school vacation instead of the two or three months which had been the norm in the past. In Zebediela in the 1970s, *koma* was no longer the prerogative of the chief, and its value was notably diminished among non-Christian youth who were progressing to higher classes in school. As Robert D Kekana, a former student at Matladi High School, recalled in an interview:

> [W]hen you go to secondary school you experience less of this "*lešoboro*" [derogatory name for an uninitiated person] thing. And especially the students from the south [meaning the Rand] would look down upon the people who had been initiated … because they associated them with backwardness.[14]

As the only secondary school in the Zebediela area until the mid-1970s, Matladi provided some space for Christian and non-Christian youth to socialise and for a more uniform youth culture to gradually develop. Furthermore, as one of the few schools with boarding facilities at a time when secondary schooling was extremely curtailed for Africans in urban areas, it attracted students not only from outlying areas in the northern Transvaal but also from Pretoria and the Witwatersrand further south.[15] For some urban-based parents, however, sending their children to rural schools such as Matladi was not just a question of a shortage of schools in towns but was a matter of preference: they desired to see their children growing up in an ordered rural environment where deference of youngsters to their elders was still a norm, away from the corrupting influence and turmoil of town life.

Thus urban students added a third dimension to the interaction among students at the school. Their presence almost immediately generated differences that contributed to pre-existing contours of conflict. Naturally, perhaps because of their exposure to a much more "modern" lifestyle and entertainment activities such as film, urban students were initially somewhat aloof, and saw themselves as superior to rural ones. They considered rural communities to be backward for still adhering to traditional practices such as *koma* and *bogoši* (chieftainship), practices which had arguably lost their value among most urban Africans. In contrast, rural students, like their parents, regarded urbanites with some suspicion, and were particularly resentful of what they perceived to be corrupt habits such as *tsotsi* (gangster) tendencies among urban boys. On top of that, local students 'regarded the boarders as strangers who were encroaching on their territory and their school... [and] so they felt they couldn't be intimidated by trespassers'.[16] Thus the resentment among students stemmed not only from the urban/rural dichotomy, but also from the insider/outsider mentality. However, by its very nature, the school set-up fostered contact and friendships across these dividing lines.

There were numerous aspects in which the students found common ground for interaction and cooperation. The exposure of most urban students to Christianity made it possible for them to fraternise more with rural Christian students than with non-Christians. Nonetheless, irrespective of their backgrounds, the students met under the same roof in the classroom context and they were taught by the same teachers. Perhaps most importantly, enthusiasm for sport at school – especially soccer, netball, and softball – as well as for debating, provided additional common experiences for all students, whether urban or rural, initiated or uninitiated, insider or outsider. Nevertheless, the Soweto Uprising came a bit too early for the students at Matladi to have a common response.

## Conclusion

The 1976 Soweto students' uprising came at a time when the fostering of a sense of common identity among the students in secondary schools and universities in the countryside, especially in institutions with boarding facilities, was still in its infancy. The pattern of conflict between urban students and local students indicates that a potential bridge existed between the two groups, but it broke down in the end. The news of the Soweto students' uprising and pressure from the urban students for camaraderie on the part of their rural counterparts led to a rupture of the evolving solidarity and the resurgence of earlier prejudices and mistrust. If the 1976 Soweto students' uprising happened too early for rural youth to find it meaningful to their experiences, the political upheavals of the mid-1980s happened at the right moment, when generational consciousness had become much more deeply rooted among these youngsters who by then had emerged as major social actors with a clearer political mission than their predecessors. But that is a story for another occasion.

## Endnotes

1   This essay is based on a chapter in my Master's degree research report, completed in 1995, as well as on a rereading of the fieldwork and archival material research conducted in 1994. See, SP. Lekgoathi, Reconstructing the History of Educational Transformation in a Rural Transvaal Chiefdom: The radicalisation of teachers in Zebediela from the early 1950s to the early 1990s, MA by Coursework and Research Report, University of the Witwatersrand, Johannesburg, 1995.

2   Bundy borrowed this concept from Mannheim's notion of "social generation". See, for example, C. Bundy, Street Sociology and Pavement Politics: Aspects of youth and student resistance in Cape Town, 1985, *Journal of Southern African Studies*, 1987, 13(3), April, 303–30.

3   B. Hirson, *Year of Fire, Year of Ash –The Soweto Revolt: Roots of a revolution?* London: Zed Books, 1979; South African Institute of Race Relations (hereafter SAIRR), *A Survey of Race Relations in South Africa, 1977*. Johannesburg: SAIRR, 1978, 64, 71; *Rand Daily Mail*, 16 September 1977, cited in SAIRR, *Race Relations Survey 1977*, 1978, 73–4.

4   Interview with Lebogang (Lebs) Mphahlele by Sekibakiba Peter Lekgoathi, Johannesburg, 6 December 1994.

5   Ibid.

6   Interview with Hector Mathekgana by Sekibakiba Peter Lekgoathi, Moletlane, Zebediela, 7 June 1994.

7   Interview with Mathekgana, 1994.

8   Interview with Alfred Matlaila by Sekibakiba Peter Lekgoathi, Groothoek Hospital, Zebediela, 10 June 1994; Interview with Matonkana J. Madisha by Sekibakiba Peter Lekgoathi, Magatle Village, Zebediela, 22 May 1994.

9   Ibid.

10  Principal's Log Book, Matladi Secondary School, 1947–1979, entry dated 29 September 1976.

11  Ibid, entry dated 20 October 1977.

12  Idem.

13  P. Delius, Mapping Histories of Rural Education: Where tradition and modernity clash, *Matlhasedi*, 1992, 11, 1, July.

14  Interview with Robert D. Kekana by Sekibakiba Peter Lekgoathi, Mogoto Village, Zebediela, 10 April 1994.

15  Boarders' Admission Register, Matladi High School, 1956–1979.

16  Interview with Madisha, 1994.

Sekibakiba Peter Lekgoathi (PhD, University of Minnesota) is an associate professor of History at the University of the Witwatersrand, Johannesburg. He has published widely on Ndebele ethnicity; the history of the SABC's African language radio and its workings; the ANC's Radio Freedom; education; the politics of knowledge production, with specific reference to the relationship between white anthropologists and black research assistants in southern Africa; as well as on popular protests in parts of South Africa during the 1980s and early 1990s.

# CHAPTER 10

# MY JOURNEY, OUR JOURNEY
## Activism at Ongoye University

---

### MAKHOSAZANA XABA

I had said I wasn't gonna' write no more poems like this.
But the dogs are in the streets.
It's a turn around world where things all too
quickly turn around.
It was turned around so that right looked wrong.
It was turned around so that up looked down.
It was turned around so that those who marched
in the streets
with bibles and signs of peace became enemies
of the state
and risks to National Security;
so that those who questioned the operations of
those in authority
on the principles of justice, liberty and equality
became the vanguard of a communist attack.

from *A Poem for Jose Campos Torres* by Gil Scott-Heron

When I arrived at the University of Zululand, popularly known as Ongoye (or Ngoye) University, in 1982, I was feeling proud of myself because although I was an older student – having already completed a four-year General Nursing and Midwifery Diploma at Edendale College – I was choosing education instead of a salaried nursing job. The excitement of being a full-time student suggested unending possibilities for me. In 1984 when I was expelled and I left the university without having completed my degree, I was even prouder of myself than when I started, but the reason was different – I had stood up for what I believed was right; I had followed my conscience – my political conscience.

In order to better understand what happened in Ongoye in the early 1980s it becomes important to look at the broader geographical area and understand its politics. As students at the university we were not immune to the influences of our surroundings. We analysed them, reacted and actively responded to them and in turn also contributed to them by creating what we believed was right. As students at the university we also all had our individual pasts. Pasts that had moulded us as groups and as individuals in one way or the other. Pasts we had moulded in individual and collective chosen ways.

So who was I politically? What had influenced me *before* going to Ongoye University that made me choose to be a student activist? The politics of Natal (now KwaZulu-Natal) – where I was born and bred – has had a long history, but I will focus only on the period that shaped me. Put differently, what I *allowed* to shape me. I will start by stepping backwards just a little. After finishing primary school in Ndaleni where we lived, my parents sent me to Pholela High School in 1971 for further education. Pholela was a mixed boarding school run by Scottish missionaries, located close to the so-called Drakensberg mountains, where it snowed every winter. uMahwaqa is the mountain range that seemed to tower ominously above the school grounds, distant as it was.

As a new student, I was placing my curious self through as many activities as possible. It was during a debating session that I heard the name Stephen Bantu Biko. I do not remember any of the points these debaters were making, what stood out for me was this Biko person debaters on one side were so passionate about. What stood out for me were the points they made about the importance of black consciousness, black pride, black confidence, black self-determination. And yes, that "black is beautiful". There was mention during this debate of a student organisation, South African Students' Organisation (SASO), that had been formed just two years before, with Biko as one of its important leaders.

After the debate I checked my dictionary for the word "self-determination" because I knew the meanings of consciousness, pride, confidence and beauty but not "determination". Something shifted inside me and it is very difficult to describe that shift. Intellectually, it was only then that I understood *racism as a system*. I awakened to this powerful realisation in a deeply emotional way. I understood the roots of the hatred I had experienced when meted out by Indians and white people. I was thirteen years old and things were never the same again in my mind: how I thought about myself, my family and black people in general. But, of course, life continued as normal. Beyond the debating society there wasn't much room for the conversation on racism even though there was fertile ground for it.

For instance, we were taught all the subjects in Afrikaans except for Mathematics and Physical Science which were taught in English. We often joked that the Afrikaners were not smart enough to teach Mathematics. A black woman, Mrs Khonyane, who was the wife of the boarding master, taught us Mathematics, and Physical Science was taught by the English-speaking Mr Johnson. Our corridor-like library had so few isiZulu books that I read all of them before the end of my first year. We did not need to understand Black Consciousness beyond what we witnessed. The ridiculousness of having black children taught in Afrikaans was looking us in the face. The attempt by the missionaries to institutionalise Scottish culture was with us through the brass band, whose perennial presence and performance at major school events was the school's pride, and the boys-only-ness of the band did not go unnoticed by some of us.

I remember thinking then about the myriad ways in which racial supremacy is "institutionalised", even though I did not know the word then. It's the little, seemingly innocuous things that are most dangerous: the school library and the books it contained; the insistence that we be taught in Afrikaans; and, our teachers – mostly white at a blacks-only school – who were for me the loudest messages of the school's intentions. I did not have a historical and political understanding of the role of missionaries then but I knew it felt wrong to me. Besides the debate, there was no other avenue I ever heard of in those three years where, as students, we could discuss politics. This was soon to change when my parents sent me to Inanda Seminary for my matric.

Inanda Seminary, I was soon to learn, had a proud history: missionary as well but focused on the education of the girl child. This of course was a political standpoint, one that challenged the perennial sexism in our lives. The "openly political" conversations in class and during assembly simply said that the personal is political, although that was not the slogan we used then. In the library I came upon the African Writer series, many more books written in isiZulu, and some by women from across the world. This library was as different from the Pholela library as night is from day. My love for books was entrenched.

In addition, during the 1975 International Women's Year, 8 March was declared and celebrated by the United Nations as International Women's Day. I was so excited by this idea that I made a drawing of women marching and submitted it to our school journal *EzaKwa MaEdwards*. Terrible as the art was, my teacher took my submission and it ended up on the back cover. Clearly she valued the idea of the drawing more than its artistic aspects. That was the year I was no longer just black and proud. I was black, woman, and proud. That was also the year I wrote my first letter to a political prisoner on Robben Island, in solidarity with my friend whose brother-in-law was serving time there.

The year 1975 was also the year when the Inkatha movement revived itself publicly. I remember a few conversations we had in class and among ourselves when we heard the news. I remember the discomfort we felt about its essence: the tribal nucleus of organising. We saw it as collusion with the apartheid regime's "homeland" system. As young women we were learning about becoming world citizens not "Zulus". We were also concerned about what seemed like the traditionalist nature of the organisation, one that valued men more than it did women. It was problematic to the point of being dangerous, politically. Little did I know then how just under a decade later I was to come face to face, literally, with men of Inkatha.

I first heard about what had happened in Soweto on June 16 while listening to Springbok Radio, alone at home. My parents and siblings had gone to school for the day. I had been in bed since January. Springbok Radio had become my closest friend because it carried me away from the bed I could not leave, to the whole of the country, and I became addicted to news, and to stories. And so June 16 unfolded, spread through the country, as days and months went by. I was on top on the news. My analysis was cobbled from Springbok Radio, Radio Zulu, my father's newspapers and my mother's magazines. Emotionally and politically, I became another person, once again. I knew then how far the racist government was prepared to go. The more I understood that the clearer it became to me that doing nothing was irresponsible. But, what was I to do?

I arrived at Edendale College in March of 1977. In September Steve Biko died. My cohort known as "Group 4/77" (April being the month we formally began our training, after a month of preparation) had many who had been at university in 1976 and had not returned. We were lumped together and labelled as the rebellious ones. Yes, we spoke our minds in class but we did our work in the wards too and there wasn't much room for doing and talking politics there.

The sadness I felt at Biko's death did not weigh as heavily on me as the loneliness and anger did. Through some meandering route I found relief, consolation and hope at the Edendale Lay Ecumenical Centre, where Ben Dikobe Martins worked as a resident artist and an informal librarian of banned and underground books and literature. The list of books I read and tapes I listened to is too long to list. I will only say this: I read about revolutions in many parts of the world and listened to political speeches of note. But, I also read fiction, like Bessie Head's *Maru*. I often returned books, like Gramsci's, without having understood half of what I had read, but I was hungry for more and Ben's library never disappointed. I first listened to Martin Luther King's *I have a dream* speech, as well as Gil Scott-Heron's, *A Poem for Jose Campos Torres*, whose simple yet memorable lines have lived with me since then because they captured so accurately our political situation. I read books on women workers' struggles in Mexico and about Marxism and Leninism; the range seemed limitless. I became a weekly visitor loaning and returning books and tapes all of which injected into me a political and social growth spurt and consciousness beyond my wildest dreams. Most importantly I understood at a very deep level that racism, sexism and classism exist all over the world, that South Africa was not unique, and that people everywhere had had to fight against these in order to see change. Such was my breadth of political and social consciousness then when I went on to Ongoye University.

Four major personal and political events confronted me during my first year at university. They were major for me, in *my* journey. First was my decision to join the Azanian Students' Organisation (AZASO). I don't even remember how I first heard of it but I joined without much thought because it simply made sense. I attended many meetings on campus, most of which took place at the men's residences, and very often I was the only woman. During these meetings we talked about our lives as students but, most importantly, about politics – the state of the nation countrywide. I was thirsty and enjoyed these discussions so I went each time, feeling sorry for myself when I missed a session. One day I asked the question about the minimal and infrequent attendance of female students at these meetings and Mmuso Mosery threw the question back at me and suggested simply: 'Why don't *you* organise them?' The many questions that ran through my head kept returning to one answer: of course, he is right; even if you do it badly, it's worth doing, it's meaningful, it's important, it makes perfect sense. So I did.

Second, I have *never*, to this day, forgotten the day we gathered in the main hall to listen to Phumzile Mlambo who had come from the University of Natal to address the student body, the day I first heard the word "neo-colonialism". The fully packed hall was ablaze with emotion, we came alive. Everything she said, every way she said it, and her presence on stage, were practical manifestations of the black women I imagined we were meant to be. Her visit strengthened my will to do the "organising of female students" I had taken on, although I kept feeling as if I was not making much headway.

Third, the Koornhof Bills were introduced by the apartheid government, a clear sign that they planned to oppress black people even further. Fourth, a parcel bomb killed Ruth First in Mozambique, in August. When we talked about this in our groups I became more and more simultaneously fearful and resolute. The apartheid machinery was everywhere and ruthless. I too could die. Was I prepared?

The challenge of organising female students was not to be the last one from Mosery. In 1983 he and others in the student leadership told me that it would be a good idea for me to talk at the Steve Biko commemoration meeting in the main hall, the one Phumzile had spoken at the year before. No amount of protesting let me off *that* hook. In fact they told me how we would write the paper together, how I did not have to memorise it, how I would have to do a few dry runs and read it aloud to myself just to feel confident, and how in fact being just slightly older than average second-year students was an advantage because the students would take me seriously, and how in fact I knew enough already to make this work.

The introduction of the Koornhof Bills produced a national response that led to heightening of mobilisation of the progressive people within the country, leading to the formation of the United Democratic Front (UDF) on 20 August 1983. We fundraised for some of us to attend the launch. Looking back, the formation of the UDF was like a line drawn among black people to make very clear who was on which side of the political spectrum. It was not long after that we started hearing rumours that Chief Gatsha Mangosuthu Buthelezi, founder of Inkatha, was planning to use the main hall on the campus for the commemoration of King Cetshwayo's death.

We protested as loudly as we could, we demonstrated on campus, we talked to management without success. The tension among us heightened, and honestly, until then I had not been aware of just how many students on campus were in fact members of Inkatha. Nor was I aware of how committed they were. As a last resort, we decided to apply for an interdict to stop the meeting. The tensions among us students intensified as the Inkatha-aligned students made it clear that they were in support of the celebrations scheduled for Saturday 29 October. On the night of October 28, we met until very late into the night, trying to plan without knowing what the morning would deliver.

The singing sounds of war were unmistakably heading in our direction – towards the women's residence – as early as eight in the morning on that fateful Saturday. A few of us ran outside to look because it soon became clear that these assegai and knobkerrie wielding men had marched past the main hall. What were they coming to our residence for so early in the morning? Why had the security guard let them in? They did not sound like participants coming to a celebratory event. In innocent curiosity we stepped outside to watch the men advance. I was one of the first few to be hit by the angry men. The one who hit me used an *imvubu*, which landed on the small of my back – making a scar that lived visibly for many years. We, bewildered, ran back to the hostel to hide, to watch through the windows, to plead with security to lock the main doors.

We soon realised these were not just a few men who had wandered in the direction of the women's residence. There were hundreds of them; it was an army of men. We saw from the window how they approached the men's residences. Chaos ensued. The students who tried to hit back and drive the army away from the residences with the stones they found were driven back into the buildings by the sheer numbers. We saw the Inkatha men enter the buildings, running as if at war with their equals. We heard the screams and the cries. It was all so surreal. We stood there watching another "Soweto" unfold right in front of us, only this time it was hundreds of armed black men attacking unarmed students on their very campus and following them into their rooms to injure and kill them.

In the afternoon, after it was clear that the warring men had left, we walked outside the residence and saw some students sitting on the hill. They had run out of the buildings for dear life and climbed the hill. We took food from the dining room, walked up the hill to deliver it and assure them that the danger had gone, that it was safe for them to return. That afternoon an emergency meeting was called by the student leadership. Those who could meet, met outside the women's residence because we could not handle the shock of what had just happened at the men's residences. The emergency meeting agreed to elect a seven-person Crisis Committee. I was one of those elected. Our first task was to visit Empangeni Hospital where the injured had been taken.

The shocking news of the five dead awaited us. After the hospital visit two of us were tasked with writing a report to send to the newspapers the following day. We wrote this in my room, as we still couldn't bring ourselves to go to the men's. We did not sleep that night of 29 October 1983. A night I was to relive in my dreams for decades to come.

The university descended into a mess. So many years later it's hard to retell the story in sequence and with some cohesion. What I remember with pain and anger is the way in which the rector and vice-chancellor Professor AC Nkabinde received the Crisis Committee when we wanted to talk about what had happened. The senior management at the university seemed to have the impression that we – the students who protested – were responsible for the deaths and the injuries. There were only two lecturers we could rely on for support, and we worked with them through that tough period. In time sympathetic parents, students in other universities – the University of Natal in particular – and community leaders who were as shocked and alarmed by the massacre, offered their support. Some of the community leaders initiated crisis committees and worked with us to deal with the aftermath of the massacre. Support for families whose children had died was crucial. I remember, in particular, Reverend Wesley Mabuza of the Methodist Church, who was then based in Durban. He was present at most of the meetings and took a leadership role in engaging with the communities and the management at the university. The power of the moment – the formation of the UDF with its clear agenda of progress politics – also worked in our favour. The lines were clearly drawn.

A commission of enquiry was established and many of us, the members of the Crisis Committee in particular, were instructed to speak to the enquiry. Soon after the hearings were completed, we, the seven members of the Crisis Committee, were expelled from the university. Luckily we had completed the first semester of 1984. So it was that two and half years after my arrival at the university I was made to leave for having stood up for what was right. For the first time after my political awakening, I too was prepared to die for what was right.

The year 2016 does not only mark 40 years since the Soweto Uprising, it also marks one hundred years since the opening of the very first university for black people in southern Africa, the one later renamed "Fort Hare". The long story of activism and fundraising for the university way beyond South Africa's borders is admirable, and the results of its opening in 1916 became the living, breathing evidence of self-determination by the black people of that time. Reading the history of Fort Hare from various sources confirms that the youth of each generation are the change agents; they plant the seeds of the world they want by acting resolutely, and, in some instances, they are prepared to die. Universities often become the training ground where the youth try out their ideas, come into their own, and where they dream.

I have told the story of my political development above as a way to make the point that very few people arrive at commitment to activism overnight; it is a journey. Some parts of the journey may be unconscious and mundane while others may be dramatic and painful. But, during the journey, as individuals, we make choices. We say "yes", "no", or "maybe" to something. We say "yes", "no", or "maybe" by acting or by not acting. We may speak out about our choices or we may be silent. It is in how we *act* them out that we speak the loudest. My story and my journey are similar to the journeys of many others who grew up in Natal or were in Natal for their education. The specifics may differ but the overarching political context is the same, and so we journeyed, our individual consciences and choices paving our routes.

Makhosazana Xaba is the author of two poetry collections, *These Hands* (Timbila, 2005) and *Tongues of their Mothers* (UKZN Press, 2008), as well as *Running and Other Stories* (Modjaji Books, 2013), which won the SALA Nadine Gordimer Short Story Award in 2014. She is the co-editor of an anthology of short stories, *Queer Africa: New and Collected Fiction* (MaThoko's Books, 2013), which won the 26th Lambda Literary Award in the fiction anthology category in 2014. She holds an MA in Creative Writing (with distinction) from the University of the Witwatersrand. She is a feminist activist at heart with years of experience in the women's health sector, philanthropy and the struggle against apartheid.

# CHAPTER 11

# 'LET'S BEGIN TO PARTICIPATE FULLY NOW IN POLITICS'[1]

## Student politics, Mhluzi Township, 1970s

### TSHEPO MOLOI

F
ive weeks after students in Soweto took to the streets in 1976 demonstrating against the imposition of Afrikaans as a medium of instruction in African schools, Mhluzi township in Middelburg (Mpumalanga) erupted. The demonstration was spearheaded mainly by students from Sozama Secondary School and inaugurated a period of intense protest against schools and government institutions that continued episodically from July 1976 to May 1978. Various scholars, political commentators and activists have, over the years, extensively researched South African student politics,[2] but the struggles in Mhluzi township have been largely ignored.

The Cillie Commission of Enquiry, headed by the then Supreme Court Judge President, Judge Piet Cillie, noted that 'in comparison with other regions, *the Eastern Transvaal* saw very little rioting. Moreover, the riots were not of a very high intensity'.[3] Similarly, Holden and Mathabatha argued that 'the protests of 16 June 1976 had little impact *in the region*'.[4] This was true for many areas in the region. Although some of the students in some areas in the Eastern Transvaal attempted to rise and demonstrate, this was largely sporadic and was quickly quelled by the police.[5]

In this chapter I will argue that the reason for the intense demonstrations in Mhluzi was largely because some of the students, particularly the leaders, had been introduced to politics prior to the uprising. This enabled them to organise and sustain the demonstrations in the township. Furthermore, I will show that the role played by teachers adhering to the Black Consciousness (BC) philosophy, and students who studied outside South Africa, was crucial in conscientising some of the young people in Mhluzi.

## Mhluzi township

Mhluzi is an African township in Middelburg, Mpumalanga province (formerly Eastern Transvaal). Middelburg, formerly called Nazareth, was proclaimed a new district in 1872.[6] Coalfields were the main employment centres. Over the years it grew steadily. By the 1930s the African township, Mhluzi (meaning gravy in IsiZulu), had already been established.[7] Unlike its neighbouring township Kwaguqa, in Witbank, Mhluzi seemed to have been a relatively quiet township politically.[8] This changed, however, in the early 1970s. During this period, many young people in various townships across the country were being introduced to the teachings of BC. BC adherents such as teachers and activists in the townships played a pivotal role in developing young people politically, and this caused some of the young people to develop radical attitudes and to begin to question the status quo.[9] Students in Mhluzi were no different. However, in addition, the young people in Mhluzi township had been conscientised and organised by Cowen Ntuli,[10] a young person who was studying in Swaziland at the beginning of the 1970s.

Cowen was the son of a minister in the Nazerene Church in Mhluzi. Ntuli Senior had sent Cowen to study in Swaziland. While there he joined the Pan Africanist Congress (PAC) and its military wing, the Azanian People's Liberation Army (APLA).[11] On visits home, he recruited some of the young people in the township to APLA. One of his recruits was January (Che) Masilela.[12] He also organised clandestine meetings where he conscientised some of the other young people living in the township. Garth Mngomezulu, who fled the country in the early 1980s to join the ANC (African National Congress) and MK (Umkhonto we Sizwe, Spear of the Nation) in exile, recalls:

> By the time we were doing our Form Three [Grade 10], we had comrades like the late Cowen Ntuli ... He was studying in Swaziland and he came back. He had just finished his matric, his O-level, in Swaziland. He came back home. He is actually the guy who organised us. He said 'Comrades, let's begin to participate fully now in politics'.

To conceal their activities, they used the Nazarene church, with Cowen's father's blessing, as their venue. Mngomezulu adds:

Well, we started with him. We used the very same church of his parents.
The father and mother didn't have any problem. Every evening we used to
have meetings there where he used to address us and other comrades like
Somthuli Kubheka … comrade Jabu Sindane, comrade Mandla Tlayi Sebolai.
Those are the people that actually groomed us politically.[13]

This group of activists kept to themselves and the more curious young people in the
township were inspired by the unity the group demonstrated. They wished to be part
of this group. Johannes (Ka) Shabangu, who was a student at Sozama, remembers:

There were those older people we were looking at or upon as an inspiration
and some of them had done their teacher's training courses and some were
… finishing their Form 4 [Grade 11] and matric. Seeing them gathering,
whether they were five or three or two … Sometimes we wondered 'what
are they talking about?' And very interestingly they kept the group together.
At some point I said 'No, this must be a very interesting group'. I wished at
some point I could find myself in that group.[14]

Shabangu did not get the opportunity to join the group, because in 1978 he fled the
country into exile where he joined MK. His journey into exile was, however, facilitated
by one of the members of the group, Jabu Sindane.[15]

Many young people in the township, especially those who were not privy to the
clandestine meetings at the Nazarene church, received their political education from the
recently-graduated teachers from the Universities of the North (Turfloop) and Zululand
(Ngoye). In the 1970s universities designated for black students only, particularly
Turfloop, became strongholds for BC adherents. In 1972 more than one thousand
students at Turfloop were either expelled or suspended following the speech by one of
the leading figures in the South African Students' Organisation – a BC-aligned students'
organisation – and this caused protests in black universities across the country.[16]

Mandla Seloane was one of the students who were expelled from Turfloop for
participating in the strike protests against the expulsion of Onkgopotse Tiro in 1972. He
returned to Mhluzi and, because of a dearth of teachers in the area, he was immediately

offered a teaching position at Sozama Secondary School. Together with Thuli Kubheka, a young graduate from Ngoye, he wasted no time and began to politicise his students.[17] By 1975 some of the students from Sozama were seriously engaging in political discussions. In the same year they formed the Mhluzi Students' Organisation (MSO) and affiliated to the South African Students' Movement (SASM)[18].

SASM was largely made up of senior students in secondary and high schools.[19] They were not directly affected by Afrikaans as a medium of instruction[20] and thus it took some time before they actively participated in the struggle against Afrikaans. Nieftagodien argues that after 'the struggle against Afrikaans had asserted itself as a critical issue in Soweto ... and was being addressed by a growing number of organisations, including the Black Consciousness Movement, SASM inevitably entered the fray".[21] Taking their cues from their parent body, members of MSO began to discuss the issue of Afrikaans. They were against the department's ruling that Afrikaans should be used, together with English, as a compulsory teaching language. Like other students across the country, students at Sozama could not cope with learning in Afrikaans. Shabangu explains:

> I mean, at school we were forced to be taught in Afrikaans. Before 1976 it
> had felt normal but it was difficult to do Mathematics in Afrikaans; to do
> History in Afrikaans; to do Geography in Afrikaans; to do Religious Studies
> in Afrikaans. We virtually turned to become black Afrikaners ... When
> they said the whole uprising was about refusing to be taught in Afrikaans it
> was a welcoming suggestion to some of us, to say 'away with this'.[22]

In May members of MSO attended a meeting organised by SASM at Wilgespruit, on the West Rand, where the decision was taken to support the schools affected by the policy of Afrikaans.[23] It is surprising, however, that young people in Mhluzi did not immediately take to the streets after their counterparts in Soweto started demonstrating on 16 June. Four weeks passed before they demonstrated. It is not clear what the reason for this was, but it is possible that the gradual movement into exile of some of the students, especially influential figures within the MSO, might have played a role. Mngomezulu recalls that 'the first group of our age who left the country left in 1975'.[24] At this stage many of the students were fleeing to Swaziland in search of a better education.[25]

## Mhluzi erupts

On 20 July 1976, the day schools re-opened after the mid-year winter holidays, Mhluzi was on fire. Recalling the day students from Sozama took to the streets to demonstrate in solidarity with their counterparts in Soweto and elsewhere in the country, Shabangu explained:

> I did throw some stones. I did put some boulders in the road. I did
> contribute in burning some tyres to prevent the armed personnel from
> going through to some of the schools.[26]

According to Ben Mokoena, the MSO called all the students to a meeting in an open field to discuss their plan of action. After deliberating, students agreed that they should march to town to protest the killing of students in Soweto and the use of Afrikaans in schools. Alas, the police had heard about the students' plan. They rushed to the township and stopped the students from marching to town. A fight broke out between the police and students. A number of marchers were shot and injured. Mokoena and some of the student leaders were arrested.[27] Possibly in retaliation, the students, then joined by non-school-going youth, attacked government properties.

An excerpt from the Cillie Commission report provides a detailed account of what happened:

> 20 July 1976: The schools reopened. A group of scholars marched through
> Mhluzi, disturbing the peace. Bantu Affairs Administration Board offices,
> a clinic and vehicles, including an ambulance, a bus and a police vehicle,
> were pelted with stones. They set fire to a train depot and a bus, and
> attacked four BAAB's constables. The South African Police fired a number
> of shots. The rioters continuously gave the Black Power salute.[28]

In the following days, students turned their anger toward school buildings in the township. The Cillie Commission reported that on 6 August 1976 at 03h00, Thusanang, Reatlegile and Manyano schools were set on fire. The total damage amounted to R86 000.[29]

The situation in the township was tense. Students refused to return to school until their colleagues were released from detention. On the morning of 21 September, about 100 youths congregated in front of the magistrate's court in town to support the detained students, who were due to appear in court. When the police ordered them to disperse, they refused. The police responded by shooting tear gas. Angrily, the youth returned to the township where they assaulted people, possibly those who were perceived to be collaborators, and pelted a bus and a house with stones.[30]

In December the detained students were granted bail and some of them decided to leave the country and go into exile. Mokoena, who was transported by Jabu Sindane, remembers that they 'went through Piet Retief, went over the fence and stayed for a few days in teacher Mbatha's house in Swaziland, not far from the border gate between South Africa and Swaziland'.[31]

Clearly, by this stage the demonstrations by students in Mhluzi had shifted from educational grievances. Students were now protesting against the apartheid system in general. To challenge this system, they galvanised their parents to oppose the local administration. This was not peculiar to Mhluzi. After the government had abandoned its Afrikaans policy on 6 July, students in Soweto, initially led by the Action Committee and, later the Soweto Students' Representative Council, turned to their parents and workers for support in attacking the economy of the country.[32]

## Students and civic politics

The December holidays failed to dampen the students' spirit and momentum. In the new year they continued where they had momentarily left off. But now their grievances included rent hikes and lack of social services in the township. Shabangu explains:

> So we participated against that background. But also in the process it began to touch issues like we want to move from these small four rooms and get bigger houses, we want to move away from this bucket system that was still in our township to get the sewerage system ... we want to have recreational facilities and so on.[33]

A national newspaper reported that in Mhluzi 'most of the houses have no sanitation and no lighting … [and] communal toilets are available in some parts'.[34] In spite of these conditions, the township's administration board was set on increasing rent by more than 50%. In some instances the increases were very steep: rent for four-roomed houses increased from R5.20 to R14.50, that is, nearly 300%.[35] For many of the residents in the township, particularly the low-skilled employees and domestic workers whose earnings ranged between R20 and R30 a month, this was unbearable. Students from Sozama took up the fight on behalf of their parents, demonstrating against rent increases.[36] The police responded heavy-handedly. On 30 April 1978 police used tear gas to disperse students from Sozama, detaining students and charging them with sabotage.[37]

At this stage a number of youth from Mhluzi decided to flee the country to join the banned political organisations in exile. Shabangu recruited 11 young people to flee with him but some of them "chickened out" and when they left they were only four.[38] Undoubtedly, the constant and rapid movement of young people into exile caused the students' demonstrations to recede. Also, the sentencing of Isaac Sikhumbuzo Mtsweni in 1978 to five years' imprisonment[39] probably had an impact on the young activists in the township.

## Conclusion

Although young people in Mhluzi began to demonstrate relatively late, they were able to sustain their demonstrations until mid-1978. I have contended that this was mainly due to their early politicisation. At the beginning of the 1970s some of the young people in the township started engaging in clandestine political discussions led by a young person who had close connections with a banned liberation movement in exile. In addition, some of the young people were introduced to politics by teachers who adhered to BC teachings. A year before the student uprisings, some of the students from Sozama Secondary School had formed a student body, which they used to conscientise and mobilise the rest of the student body in the township. By the time they took to the streets demonstrating in solidarity with their counterparts in Soweto and elsewhere in the country, students from Sozama were ready and fully aware of their actions. To sustain their protest, in 1977 students mobilised the community to fight against the lack of service delivery in the township and the local administration's decision to increase rents. The student uprising finally lost momentum after a number of young people decided to flee the country to join the banned liberation movements in exile.

## Endnotes

1   This quote is taken from an interview with Garth Mngomezulu by Tshepo Moloi and Sekibakiba Lekgoathi, Mhluzi, Middelburg, 12 November 2015.

2   See for example, N. Nieftagodien, *The Soweto Uprising*. Johannesburg: Jacana, 2014; H. Mashabela, *A People on the Boil: Reflections on June 16 1976 and beyond, 30th Anniversary edition*. Johannesburg: Jacana, 2006; S. Mkhabela, *Open Earth and Black Roses: Remembering 16 June 1976*. Johannesburg: Skotaville, 2001; SM. Ndlovu, The Soweto Uprising, in South African Democracy Education Trust (hereafter SADET) (ed.), *The Road to Democracy in South Africa, Volume 2, 1970–1980*. Pretoria: UNISA Press, 2007; SM. Ndlovu, *The Soweto Uprisings: Counter-memories of June 1976*. Johannesburg: Ravan Press, 1998; A. Brooks and J. Brickhill, *Whirlwind before the Storm: The origins and development of the uprising in Soweto and the rest of South Africa from June to December 1976*. London: International Defence and Aid Fund for Southern Africa, 1980.

3   Report of the Commission of Inquiry into the Riots at Soweto and Elsewhere from the 16th of June 1976 to the 28th of February 1977, Republic of South Africa, 1980, 178 (emphasis added).

4    P. Holden and S. Mathabatha, The politics of resistance: 1948–1990, in P. Delius (ed.) *Mpumalanga: History and Heritage*. Pietermaritzburg: University of KwaZulu-Natal Press, 2007, 412 (emphasis added).

5    See for example, Report of the Commission, 178-181.

6    The Founding of Middelburg, (n.d.).

7    Middelburg, Mpumalanga (1859–1996): Photographic album on Middelburg (n.d.).

8    In the early 1960s Witbank became a stronghold of the Pan Africanist Congress (PAC). See, for example, Holden and Mathabatha, The Politics, 413.

9    See, for example, T. Moloi, Bodibeng High School: Black Consciousness philosophy and students' demonstration, 1940s–1976, in *South African Historical Journal,* 2011, 63(1); P. Bonner, and N. Nieftagodien, *Alexandra: A history*. Johannesburg: Wits University Press, 2008, Chapter Nine.

10   Cowen Ntuli died in Tanzania in 1979. Steve Tshwete Local Municipality ANC's 100 years, Heroes and heroines of the struggle, 2012.

11   Pitika Ntuli, his brother, joined the PAC in 1960 and in 1963 fled the country, initially settling in Swaziland. Holden and Mathabatha, The Politics, 405-6.

12   Masilela later defected and joined the ANC and Umkhonto we Sizwe. About Masilela, see for example, SM. Ndlovu, Black Youth and Students' Exile: The revival of the liberation movement(s) in the 1970s, (unpublished paper); B. Gilder, *Songs and Secrets: South Africa from liberation to governance*. Johannesburg: Jacana, 2012.

13   Interview with Mngomezulu.

14   Interview with Johannes (Ka) Shabangu by Tshepo Moloi and Philip Bonner for the Mathews Phosa Biography Project, Sandton, 5 April 2013.

15   Ibid.

16   A. Heffernan, A History of Youth Politics in Limpopo, 1967–2003, unpublished DPhil thesis, University of Oxford, 2014, Chapter Three.

17   Interview with Ben Mokoena by Tshepo Moloi for the House of Memory Heritage Organisation, 17 February 2010.

18   For an in-depth account on SASM, see N. Diseko, The Origins and Development of the South African Students' Movement (SASM), 1968–1976, in *Journal of Southern African Studies,* 1991, 18(1).

19   Some secondary schools went only from Form 1 to Form 3, while others went from Form 1 to Form 5. High schools went from Form 1 to Form 5.

20   The government directive that Afrikaans be used as a compulsory medium of instruction applied initially only to students in Forms 1 and 2. It was to be phased in for the senior forms (3 to 5) gradually over a few years.

21   Nieftagodien, *The Soweto Uprising,* 76.

22  Interview with Shabangu.

23  Interview with Mokoena; also see Ndlovu, *The Soweto Uprising*, 339.

24  Interview with Mngomezulu (emphasis added).

25  Isaac Sikhumbuzo Mtsweni, a former teacher and court interpreter, was sentenced to five
    years in prison in 1978 for, inter alia, 'providing the youths with money to ... cross into
    Swaziland to receive "royal education" and thereafter go to Botswana, Mozambique and
    Tanzania to receive military training'. *Rand Daily Mail,* 30 September 1978.

26  Ibid.

27  Interview with Mokoena.

28  Cillie Commission report, 83.

29  Ibid., 121.

30  Ibid., 269.

31  Interview with Mokoena.

32  See Nieftagodien, *The Soweto Uprising,* 118-35.

33  Interview with Shabangu.

34  *Rand Daily Mail,* 13 June 1976.

35  *Rand Daily Mail,* 25 January 1977.

36  *Rand Daily Mail*, 27 May 1978.

37  Ibid.

38  Interview with Shabangu.

39  *Rand Daily Mail,* 9 October 1978.

Tshepo Moloi is a researcher in the History Workshop, University of the Witwatersrand. He obtained his PhD in History at the same university in 2012. He is the author of *Place of Thorns: Black political protest in Kroonstad since 1976* (Wits University Press, 2015).

# CHAPTER 12

# 'THEY WOULD REMIND YOU OF 1960'[1]

## The emergence of radical student politics in the Vaal Triangle 1972–1985

### FRANZISKA RUEEDI

In 1976, when student protests spread like wildfire through Soweto, Alexandra and other parts of the country, the African townships of the Vaal Triangle to the south of Johannesburg remained relatively quiescent. Although local students identified with the grievances of protesting students in Soweto and elsewhere, student mobilisation in the region was slow. In the aftermath of June 16, sporadic boycotts disrupted school activities in the Vaal, yet students remained unorganised. This relative lack of open confrontation in 1976 was in stark contrast to the protests that catapulted the area to the forefront of resistance politics eight years later, culminating in the Vaal Uprising of 1984. David Moisi, chairman of the local branch of the South African Students' Movement (SASM), attributes the difficulties students had in mobilising in 1976 to the impact of the Sharpeville Massacre of 1960: '[T]he Vaal was not an easy area to mobilise. In fact so much that it was easier for people to actually give you away to the security police. For fear of the state'.[2] The historical memory of state violence and repression had created an atmosphere of fear and suspicion that hampered the formation of political networks and undermined public dissent. Tsietsi Mokatsanyane, who became an active member of the Congress of South African Students (COSAS) during the 1980s and went into exile in 1984, remembers the attitude of the older generation toward confrontational politics: 'They say that "No. I don't want to see. You were not there [at the massacre in 1960] my child. I was there."'[3]

Other factors that stymied the formation of political networks and the mobilisation of local students included a lack of high schools in the Vaal, an exodus of politicised students to schools in Soweto and a history of continuous removals that added to a sense of unsettlement. Moisi left Tshepo Themba Secondary School in Residensia and went to Orlando High School in Soweto in 1975, citing a lack of classes in Mathematics and Science at matric level in the Vaal as his reason for leaving. He continued to play a vital role in student politics until late 1977, when he went into exile to join Umkhonto we Sizwe (MK). The number of students from the Vaal attending high school in Soweto remained low, yet their influence in their home area was significant. Commuting between the Vaal and Soweto they brought back with them a new radical political consciousness that had its roots in the many manifestations of Black Consciousness. It was these students who initiated early forms of protest against the daily bread-and-butter grievances of the local township population. Oupa Mareletse remembers that 'if you're attending school in Soweto you're a very sophisticated person. And because the '76 thing started in Soweto, we were always looking out for them for guidance'.[4]

## The impact of Black Consciousness in the Vaal

The Black Consciousness movement had been gaining momentum since the mid-1960s, preparing the ground for the formation of the South African Students' Organisation (SASO) in 1969 – a breakaway from the National Union of South African Students (NUSAS) – and a great variety of cultural clubs and community organisations. Tom Lodge notes that in the early 1970s Sharpeville boasted a 'lively cluster of youth organisations' such as the Vaal Youth Club, the Sharpeville Cultural and Health Club, the Sharpeville Youth Club and the Sharpeville Students' Association.[5] The most significant organisation was the Sharpeville Youth Club, established in 1972 and formally launched in 1973.[6] Its main aim was to keep young people off the streets by organising cultural events. Members of the Sharpeville Youth Club were involved in the establishment of an office of the Black People's Convention (BPC) in Vereeniging and they also contributed to the formation of the National Youth Organisation (NAYO). Matime Moshele Papane, who became a leading organiser of the United Democratic Front (UDF) in the Vaal during the 1980s, remembers the impact the Sharpeville Youth Club had on his politicisation. Papane, a teenager at that time, was introduced to the club by his neighbour Nkutseou Matsau, who was one of its leading figures. Matsau was also an executive member of the African Students' Movement (ASM), which later became the South African Students' Movement (SASM). Another leading member of the Sharpeville Youth Club was Vusi Tshabalala, who was the President of SASM in 1975 and whose brother was a close friend of Papane's. Like other young people in the Vaal, Papane keenly engaged in the debates around black emancipation. Culture and poetry in particular, Papane explains, were key in the Black Consciousness movement: 'It was writing, thinking, talking about the struggles of our people. But it wasn't activism like what the UDF brought about after 1984. It was much more an elite structure'.[7]

During this period, politically conscious youth begun to attend rallies, meetings and commemorations in Soweto. 'If you wanted to attend a big rally', Gcina Malindi emphasises, 'you had to go to Soweto'.[8] Soweto captured the imagination of young people in the Vaal. Papane expressed these sentiments in a poem entitled *Soweto Burning*, writing 'Soweto is my Soweto/ Soweto is my Africa/ Soweto die it won't/ Rise Soweto rise/ From the ashes rise/ Rise my Soweto'.[9] The poem was published in *Staffrider*, a popular magazine that aspired to give voice to the oppressed and that captured the cultural expressions and political sentiments of black people across the country. Poetry readings, drama, theatre, art, literature and music were thriving in Soweto and attracted local youth from the Vaal. Ingoapele Madingoane performed his famous poems *Black Trial* and *Africa my beginning, Africa my ending* – published in 1979 and immediately banned by the apartheid regime – widely all over Soweto. They shaped an entire generation and became a regular feature at political rallies and funerals.

Dorcas Ralitsela, a keen reader of anti-colonial literature by Chinua Achebe and Jomo Kenyatta, studied at the University of the North (Turfloop) between 1968 and 1971 when the university was a hotbed for Black Consciousness. She recalls the impact her exposure had but emphasises that her politicisation was also shaped by her experiences of poverty, repression, inequality and violence. As a young social worker in the 1970s in the Vaal, she witnessed the harsh reality of apartheid oppression and the daily struggles of the impoverished township population: 'You see, coming from Turfloop [you had] that consciousness. If you are working as a social worker you have people that have problems and difficulties. And the system does not address people's problems. And just by virtue of them being black'.[10] Dorcas Ralitsela and her husband Esau became leading African National Congress (ANC) underground operatives and civic activists in the early 1980s. They played a key role in the protests that led to the uprising of 1984. In the repressive climate of the Vaal, an assertion of blackness became symbolic of the refusal of the younger generation to submit to the fear of state violence that shaped their parents' generation's lack of political activism.

## New mobilising factors and spaces

For many young people in the Vaal the tight grip of apartheid repression and the experiences of harsh poverty and violence became intertwined with the political philosophy of Black Consciousness. In 1977, David Moisi was part of a group of students that organised a protest march against a rent increase of 35%. Several hundred local students and residents participated.[11] Oupa Mareletse, who was arrested for his participation in the protest march, recalls that:

> [M]oney was not enough. So I could identify with these issues and there were about 35 of us that attended that meeting … So and then we staged this march. We went from Zone 13 to Zone 14 [in Sebokeng]. We marched for about three kilometres before we were stopped by the police.[12]

The Vaal area had experienced rapid industrialisation and expansion during and after World War 2, which led to the building of a series of townships for the African workforce in the region, of which Sebokeng was the last to be built, in 1966. The neighbouring towns of Vereeniging and Vanderbijlpark had a reputation for being very conservative and racist while local administrators regarded the townships as examples of successful social engineering. When the manufacturing industries began to falter, retrenchments and falling living standards exacerbated the socio-economic grievances of a great majority of local residents from the late 1970s. The frequent rent increases, in particular, galvanised local residents into action. Between 1977 and 1984, rent was increased by 427%, making the Vaal the most expensive area for black people to live in. For students, rent increases had dire consequences as there was little money left to pay for textbooks, school fees, food and uniforms. Furthermore, frequent evictions, overcrowding and a lack of electricity compounded the difficult conditions under which students had to study.

In the late 1970s, three high schools – Tshepo-Themba Secondary School in Residensia, Jordan Secondary School in Evaton and Lekoa Shandu School in Sharpeville – provided the bedrock for student mobilisation in the region. During the early to mid-1980s, another three schools in Sebokeng also became hubs of political activities: Moqhaka Secondary School in Zone 11, Fundulwazi in Zone 12 and Sizanani in Zone 13 – the three zones that formed the spatial node of political activism in Sebokeng. Based on networks formed at these schools, students also began to connect to one another through church and cultural groups. The Vaal Youth Crusade, a cultural club based at the African Methodist Episcopal Church in Evaton, and the Young Christian Workers, an organisation that had become prominent in the 1970s, attracted young people and provided a platform for engaging ideas and strengthening networks. A number of student and civic leaders who played key roles during the 1980s honed their leadership, organisational and rhetorical skills in these two organisations.

One of the key turning points for student mobilisation was the funeral of Johannes Matsobane on 26 August 1978. Matsobane, a student leader and active member of SASM, had been arrested in 1977 for attempted arson of a school in Sebokeng. He was subsequently charged with sabotage and sentenced to imprisonment on Robben Island, where he died of "unnatural causes" on 9 August 1978.[13] The circumstances of his death, as well as his popularity, led a large crowd of mourners to attend his funeral in late 1978. Police dispersed the crowds with tear gas and five young men were arrested for attending an "illegal gathering".[14] Matsobane's funeral had a great impact on the radicalisation of local communities and students specifically, and the formation of political networks. It was the first large public political event in the region since the Sharpeville Massacre of 1960 and it 'gave people who had several grievances the sense that they were not alone in such grievances.'[15]

During the same year, other political activists from the area were arrested for their involvement in resistance politics and sentenced to terms on Robben Island. Significantly, some of them, including Saul Tsotetsi and Thabiso Ratsomo, were released in the early to mid-1980s. They brought with them the political influence and networks of Robben Island. Ratsomo came to play a key role in the emerging civic structure in the region – the Vaal Civic Association (VCA), while Tsotetsi became a fieldworker for the South African Council of Churches (SACC) and was a leading political activist during the mid-1980s.

In 1979 the Congress of South African Students (COSAS) was launched, and a few months later, on 21 March 1980 at the annual commemoration of the Sharpeville Massacre, a local branch was formed in the Vaal. Gcina Malindi was elected chairperson and Simon Nkoli, a prominent gay rights activist, became the first secretary.[16] Malindi argues that the establishment of COSAS was strongly influenced by the ANC's strategy for mass mobilisation. In the period 1981–82, at least two ANC underground cells were operating in the Vaal, mostly influencing the formation of civic structures but also impacting on student mobilisation in the region. The majority of early COSAS leaders were concentrated in a few politicised schools and many lived in Zone 13 in Sebokeng. In Jerry Tlhopane's view, Zone 13 was 'the home of the struggle in the Vaal'.[17] With the formation of COSAS and later the Vaal Civic Association, the growing impact of the Freedom Charter and the goals and strategies of the ANC came to dominate grassroots politics in the region. Many of the first leaders of COSAS had been conscientised by Black Consciousness but shifted towards charterism in the early 1980s. Even though the Azanian People's Organisation (AZAPO) continued to mobilise local residents, the charterist organisations began to establish a political hegemony in the townships. In contrast to organisations leaning towards Black Consciousness, such as AZAPO, the Congress movement's greatest success was in mobilising around bread-and-butter issues. COSAS activists from the Vaal began attending workshops in other areas, where they learnt new songs and strengthened their networks with student activists in other parts of the country. Songs were, at times, adapted to include the names of local heroes. For example, *uMandela ufuna amajoni/ amajoni enkululeko* was changed to *uMatsobane ufuna amajoni/ amajoni enkululeko* (Matsobane wants soldiers/ soldiers for freedom). The increasing radicalisation of students was expressed in their choice of songs that celebrated MK and in the growing importance of the toyi-toyi in rallies and street battles.

While some COSAS members emphasised that their reason for joining was their rejection of apartheid as a whole, others named educational grievances or curiosity as key factors. An end to corporal punishment and sexual harassment of female students, the scrapping of age limits, better access to resources and the demand for democratically elected Student Representative Councils were all part of the students' agenda. Mandla Mazibuko explains:

You see when I was still in primary school we could feel there was something wrong in South Africa but we didn't understand. When I went to high school I met with guys there that belonged to an organisation called COSAS. I was then recruited into COSAS due to the harsh treatment we were receiving at school. The prefect system, the beatings, and all those things.[18]

Oupa Masankane frames his initial interest in student politics differently:

We are kids and we are inquisitive and so on. We attended [a COSAS meeting]. And we hear these elder brothers talking about politics … We fill in this form, two of us. Now we are comrades. In our school there were prefects, neh. *Now* we're going to fight them![19]

In May 1982, the National Executive of COSAS took a resolution that membership of COSAS would be restricted to school-going youth. A meeting was convened in the Vaal that saw Gcina Malindi's brother Mkhambi elected as chairman. Youth congresses such as the Soweto Youth Congress and the Port Elizabeth Youth Congress, which aimed to provide a political home for the working and unemployed youth no longer catered for by COSAS, began to mushroom all over South Africa. In the Vaal an interim Vaal Youth Congress was formed in 1984, but efforts to launch it were undermined by the uprising in September 1984 and the subsequent repression and detentions.[20]

During the early 1980s COSAS struggled to sustain campaigns because of a lack of funding and the surveillance of schools. According to Gcina Malindi, '[t]he Vaal was a difficult place to operate in with the teachers who had no political background and not tolerating any such activities. The security branch [were] watching the schools very closely'.[21] Membership was small and activities were mostly restricted to protests against rent increases and the organisation of commemoration services with AZAPO. During these meetings, Malindi emphasises, students would try to politicise the older generation: '[a]nd at every meeting we will agitate for parents to be politically involved, to be in the Vaal Civic Association. Because that was the call of the ANC from 1981. To strengthen internal mass action'.[22]

In 1980 and again in 1982, COSAS held a series of meetings to discuss opposition to the frequent rent increases. The increase from R30 to R46 in 1982 was particularly steep and local residents repeatedly clashed with the African councillors of the Vaal Triangle Community Council who were responsible for announcing the rent increases. As no civic structure that could take up the socio-economic grievances of local residents existed until 1983, COSAS was in the forefront of socio-economic struggles. As Sakhiwe Khumalo emphasises, '[t]he struggle of our fathers and mothers is our struggle. We could not isolate ourselves from the struggle of the civic movement, that of bread-and-butter issues of rents because if rent increases, it affects our going to school'.[23] By 1983, triggered by educational and socio-economic grievances, the membership in the region was swelling as more and more young students joined the ranks of COSAS.

Once the Vaal Civic Association was formed in 1983, students and the civic leadership collaborated to a greater extent. COSAS was no longer in the forefront of socio-economic struggles but it supported the activities on numerous levels. In August 1984, tensions in the townships mounted when councillors announced another rent increase of R5.90. In response, the VCA called for a protest march and stay away on 3 September. What was meant to be a peaceful protest march quickly translated into a bloody and sustained uprising that claimed the lives of dozens of people. It was a turning point that heralded the beginning of the end of the apartheid regime. In its aftermath, dozens of activists were detained and a new generation of COSAS activists assumed the leadership role in the Vaal. In contrast to the first generation of COSAS activists, this group of students had been politicised in the streets and their political consciousness was no longer shaped by Black Consciousness. Their experiences of increasing police brutality radicalised many. This led to the formation of two militant underground units in 1985 and 1986, namely the Vaal Liberation Movement (VALIMO) and Ace Mates.

## Conclusion

In the aftermath of the Sharpeville Massacre of 1960, the African townships of the Vaal Triangle saw little overt political activity. Political mobilisation was slow and in contrast to Soweto and Alexandra, students were unorganised in 1976. Yet by the late 1970s and early 1980s, the collective memory of the Sharpeville Massacre was fading. The new generation of student leaders that entered high schools were no longer deterred from engaging in politics by the fear of state violence. One of these students, David Moisi, led one of the first protest marches in the area against rent increases in 1977. After the funeral of Steve Biko in September of that year, David Moisi joined the thousands of young South Africans, including his contemporary Vusi Tshabalala, who had left the country in the aftermath of the student uprisings of 1976 to join the banned liberation movements. He went into exile and returned four years later as a guerrilla in a unit of MK that successfully bombed the Sasol II plant in Secunda on 31 May 1981.[24]

Most young black South Africans remained inside the country where their politicisation was shaped by experiences of poverty, oppression, violence and discrimination. With the formation of COSAS in 1979, the establishment of a local branch of COSAS in the Vaal in 1980, and the launch of the United Democratic Front in 1983, charterism began to dominate grassroots politics in the Vaal and elsewhere. Until the formation of the Vaal Civic Association in 1983, students played a key role in organising protests against frequent rent increases. Their struggle was intimately linked to the grievances of the older generation. Suffering from rent increases, the parents' funds became increasingly tight and often there was little money left to pay for textbooks, schools fees or uniforms. Educational grievances could therefore not be separated from civic concerns.

With the banning of COSAS on 28 August 1985, the establishment of alternative structures to channel political activism of students and youth and ensure that their activism followed charterist principles, gained in importance. In 1986, the Vaal Student Congress (VASCO) was launched, followed by the Vaal Youth Congress (VAYCO) the following year. Both organisations were hampered by frequent detentions, a lack of time and the difficulties of mobilising above ground.

## Endnotes

1    Interview with Gcina Malindi by Franziska Rueedi, Johannesburg, 25 March 2010.
2    Interview with David Moisi by Franziska Rueedi, Pretoria, 13 July 2010.
3    Interview with Tsietsi (Speech) Mokatsanyane by Franziska Rueedi, Pretoria, 13 July 2010.
4    Interview with Oupa Mareletse by Franziska Rueedi, Johannesburg, 30 June 2010.
5    T. Lodge, *Sharpeville: An apartheid massacre and its consequences*. Oxford: Oxford University Press, 2011, 286.

6    N. Nieftagodien, *The Soweto Uprising*. Johannesburg: Jacana, 2015, 43.

7    Interview with Matime Moshele Papane by Franziska Rueedi, Johannesburg, 28 April 2010.

8    Interview with Gcina Malindi by Franziska Rueedi, Johannesburg, 21 July 2010.

9    *Staffrider*, 1980, 3, 1, February.

10   Interview with Dorcas Ralitsela by Franziska Rueedi, Vereeniging, 1 April 2010.

11   Blignaut, Cooper, Gordon et al., *A Survey of Race Relations in South Africa, 1977*. Johannesburg: South African Institute of Race Relations, 1978, 410.

12   Interview with Oupa Mareletse.

13   *Work in Progress*, 6 June 1978.

14   *Post*, 27 January 1979.

15   WHP AK2117, S8.4.1, Memorandum on the emergence of the VCA.

16   Gcina Malindi, Simon Nkoli, Thabiso Ratsomo and Jerry Tlhopane were among the 22 accused standing trial for their involvement in student and civic activism in what became known as the Delmas Treason Trial.

17   Interview with Pelamotse Jerry Tlhopane by Franziska Rueedi, Sebokeng, 22 November 2011.

18   Interview with Mandla Mazibuko by Franziska Rueedi, Vanderbijlpark, 22 June 2010.

19   Interview with Oupa Masankane by Franziska Rueedi, Vereeniging, 29 June 2010.

20   Interview with Themba Goba by Franziska Rueedi, Vereeniging, 18 June 2010.

21   Interview with Gcina Malindi.

22   Interview with Gcina Malindi.

23   Interview with Sakhiwe Khumalo by Franziska Rueedi, Vereeniging, 23 June 2010.

24   Together with the two other guerrillas, Johannes Shabangu and Anthony Tsotsobe, David Moisi was arrested and sentenced to death for high treason. The sentence was later commuted.

Franziska Rueedi is a postdoctoral researcher at the University of the Witwatersrand, with a focus on the history of protest and conflict between the late 1970s and mid-1990s in South Africa. She has published journal articles on popular protest, political violence and resistance during the 1980s in the Vaal Triangle (Sedibeng). She is particularly interested in political subjectivity, the relationship between overt and clandestine forms of resistance as well as the social significance of rumour in shaping patterns of conflict and political violence.

CHAPTER 13

# THE ENDS OF BOYCOTT

### PREMESH LALU

I n July 1985, thousands of students in the Western Cape walked out of classes in solidarity with students elsewhere, in thirty-six magisterial districts in South Africa, who were subjected to a state of emergency. Cutting across apartheid's Group Area divide, the student movement grew into a protracted educational crisis that culminated in the Trojan Horse Massacre in Athlone and a similarly staged state killing of two youths in Crossroads.[1] The movement of students, and the many debates about indefinite boycott, states of emergency, education and liberation, and the importance of schooling were eloquently captured in a novel by Richard Rive titled *Emergency Continued* (Readers International 1990). Rive's novel pivots on the debate between the demands of study and revolt, especially how these demands on schooling under apartheid compelled the students of its segregated institutions to inhabit purposefully the contradiction which defined every aspiration and desire for knowledge. Implicitly, the novel asks us to consider how we name the unprecedented movement of students over a period of six months, torn between the desire for education and the effects of apartheid in blocking the desire for education. Caught in the midst of a debate of whether to argue for "liberation before education" or "education before liberation", the name we grant to the actions of students is as important for the memory of 1985 as it is for how we are to think about the meaning of education in the present. This article asks how we might discover in the student movement of 1985 a memory that endures into the future, albeit not uncritically.

The 1986 end-of-year English examination paper developed by the apartheid state's Department of Education and Culture included a question on the origins of the word boycott. This attempt at ridicule and provocation corresponded to a protracted walkout of students in protest against apartheid education in July 1985 in the Western Cape. While many admitted to venturing a playful guess that it originated with the English cricketer, Geoffrey Boycott, I recall refusing to entertain what amounted to the dark sarcasm of faceless and nameless apartheid bureaucrats. Honestly, I did not know the answer. The Irish land agent Captain Charles C. Boycott from whom the tactic of "boycott" draws its name would equally be anathema to the students who took up the struggle against apartheid education in the 1980s. That is because his name, and the tactic that it called forth, would be inadequate for explaining the micropolitics that unfolded in the student movement in 1985 in Cape Town.

If micropolitics serves to rename the movement of students in 1985, it is not because it is a form of politics on a minor scale. On the contrary, micropolitics, as Brian Massumi maintains, is an art of emitting interruptive signs, triggering the cues that attune bodies while activating their capacities differentially.[2] Put simply, micropolitics works at the level of potential and at the level of affect. To the extent that students in 1985 had in view the states of emergency declared by the apartheid state, their movement is best understood as acting upon the very notion of schooling. My argument in what follows is two-fold. Firstly, I wish to suggest that to call the student movement of 1985 a movement of boycott is to withdraw from the target of student protests, namely schooling. Secondly, I want to argue against the use of the word boycott to describe the student movement, mainly because this is a term of disciplinary reason, one that seeks to kill the traces of the spirit of that movement to think the apparatus of the school and the project of schooling as productive.[3]

## The National Education Crisis Committee meeting and an end to the boycott

In March 1986, approximately 5 000 delegates drawn from student movements, civic organisations and parent-teacher-student associations assembled in the city of Durban for the National Education Crisis Committee (NECC) meeting. The matter on the table was the end of the schools boycott that had spread through South African townships for extended periods during the mid-1980s.

For Cape Town delegates, the two-day journey to Durban was punctuated by much debate and disagreement on the call by the Soweto Parents Crisis Committee to end what had been widely known as the schools boycott. There was much preparation among students in anticipation of the encounter with Vusi Khanyile's NECC committee. In the area of Athlone, for example, there were referenda at schools that formed the core of the Athlone Students' Action Committee to gauge student attitudes.[4] All of this, however, was thrown into sharp relief as delegates arrived in Durban. Delegates were hurriedly whisked off to a new meeting venue following an attack on the offices of the NECC in which two activists were alleged to have been killed. To avert any further danger to delegates, it had been decided to move the meeting to the township of Chatsworth where discussions on the finality of the question of the schools boycott would be conducted through the night. An air of doubt hovered above the proceedings as students questioned reports of the events at the Diakonia offices in central Durban earlier in the day. Many felt uncertain, believing that the report may have been a ploy to move the discussion to end the boycott through in haste, leaving little time for deliberation. As suspected, the resolution to end the boycott was tabled at the crack of dawn, with half the delegates asleep, and the remainder, too exhausted to participate.

Perhaps, by recalling this highly charged situation in which the end of the schools boycott was secured, we are also compelled to enquire into the sources of anxiety articulated by students in March 1986. There was admittedly a sense of relief that the preceding months of pitched battles with police and security forces were drawing to a close. The student movement appeared exhausted, aimlessly adrift in places, and nowhere close to realising the initial aims that catalysed the boycott in the first place. Yet, the demand for the end of corporal punishment at schools, for an end to the state of emergency, for the release of political prisoners, and for the introduction of a deracialised education system that did not merely reproduce forms of racialised subjectivity or perpetuate a racial division of labour, seemed nowhere near being met. Against this backdrop of exhaustion, many believed privately that the time had arrived to end the schools boycott, even when many expressly held to a different view in public.

How are we to make sense of the anxiety expressed by students at the end of the boycott in 1986? Perhaps, one way to proceed is to ask what the tactic of boycott reveals about its political investment in the specific instance of the student movement in 1985, and, secondly, to enquire into what is unforeseen in the tactic of boycott that will require it to be supplemented, even surpassed, by a different order of critique.

The schools boycott that was called in July 1985 in Cape Town might allow us to think about how the tactic of boycott invests the political with particular meaning. At the outset, the boycott set out to demand the lifting of the state of emergency in 36 magisterial districts in regions other than the Western Cape. Not long after registering this demand, it was felt that the boycott would require a carefully planned and coordinated programme of education and study, under the leadership of the Student Representative Councils, and convened under the auspices of various Student Action Committees. These study sessions, involving thousands, occupied students for much of the morning session of the school day. The latter part of the day invariably saw students gather together in mass rallies with neighbouring schools, often ending in a confrontation with the security forces later in the day. The study sessions took up discussions on such themes as the South African education system, the experiments in literacy in the Nicaraguan Revolution, the nature of the apartheid state, political theory, and discussions pertaining to Mozambique, Zimbabwe and other post-independent states in Africa. In light of this demand for education, the framing of the student movement as a schools boycott seemed inappropriate for what the students of 1985 embarked upon. It could not account for the methodical displacement of a curriculum that sought to interpellate instrumentally the student into an abiding subject of racial discourse. These were the wellsprings of the national movements of people's education that were later echoed in the demand for people's power.

In fact the name boycott seemed to unduly constrain the ways in which the movement of students came to be spoken of. It needlessly supported state representations of rampaging and disinterested youth, and, in more generous accounts, as a demand that was unthinkingly driven by impulse rather than any substantive ideas for the reconstitution of politics or history. The archive of this movement, as a consequence, is the archive of documentary photographs, of declaration and demand, of public violence. It is not surprising then that this has been the scene which gave the post-apartheid era its so-called "lost generation". Neither is it unexpected that the student boycott of 1985 offers itself as a history shorn of its commitments to rethinking politics. This neglect, which I would argue must feature in a genealogy of the tactic of boycott, places before us the task of sorting out what it is that the notion of boycott condenses, even displaces.

The anxiety of those students who travelled to the conference in Durban in 1986 may indeed have reflected the dismay that their struggles were rendered in completely reductive and condensed terms. This became concentrated in an argument for an end to the boycott. And alongside this, the end of the boycott carried with it the added risk of being returned to the position of the black student – as a subject of corporal punishment and gutter education, and stripped of the desire that prompted the students into action in the first instance.

It was the discipline of history that first appeared on the scene to make sense of the student movement and to provide a reasonable justification for a retreat by students. In an essay titled *Action, Comrades, Action! The Politics of Youth-Student Resistance in the Western Cape, 1985*, the historian Colin Bundy represented the student movement in South Africa in analogous terms to youth of the Spanish Civil War through an argument about "immediatism".[5] The boycott provided the material for a rendering of the student as a sociological category, rightly, in his view, driven by impatience and through presumably overstated claims about the state being on its knees. But this recourse to immediatism was also how Bundy accounted for the fundamental flaw in the student movement. The call for indefinite boycott, and the demands for action meant that the student movement could only be viewed in the familiar terms of agency, not for its concern and opposition to the specific modalities of the exercise of power mediated through the apparatus of racialised education.

Nowhere in Bundy's narrative, however, is an effort made to come to terms with the way in which the discourse of history was at the very heart of the critique that activated students into action in the period under discussion. If Afrikaans was the mobilising point of the generation of 1976, History was the grievance of the generation of 1985. By rendering the student movement as a movement of boycott, a potentially critical intellectual formation was rendered intelligible merely as a tactical manoeuvre. Against this backdrop, the students justifiably expressed concern about being returned to a script from which they sought to depart, and where such departure seemed to offer itself as a possibility with the movement of the 1980s.

For the students who returned to school in 1986, the movement must have appeared despairingly emptied of its content. Talk of boycott seemed to become a source of suspicion. And it was clear the word boycott now carried a mocking edge aimed at students for their wild enthusiasm and overstated understanding of their capacities. The boycott would add to the figure of lack that came to define the post-apartheid discourse about youth. After 1994, this filtered into the discourse of the lost generation, a haunting sign of the diminished sense of the passage of student politics. In the aftermath of the groundswell, the political options for students were few and far between. Several joined underground military cells, many more ended up in prison, and yet others prepared themselves to latch onto populist formulations made available through a diminished programme of a reformed education system. Each option reinforced the symptom of a massive depoliticisation of education, one that continues to hold the black student in its place as a scapegoat of the nation's failures, as an object of the discourse of the lost generation and fodder for the dry season of capitalist exploitation.

If the boycott of 1985 revealed anything, it was that the tactic necessarily invested the political with a particular meaning that would make the student a subject of a discourse of lack and failure. The force behind the argument for the boycott was returned to hold the subject in its place. The predicament is beautifully elaborated in John Higgins' wonderful essay on the Connor Cruise O'Brien affair, published in a book on *Intellectuals and Politics*. Higgins offers a suggestive opening for thinking how, at the level of the tactic, the boycott reinstitutes the subject in a subordinate position.[6] If I am allowed the qualification of Higgins' essay, then we might conclude our discussion of 1985 by insisting that the call for boycott be supplemented by a further critique of disciplinary reason.

## University boycotts in the 1970s

The need for this supplementary critique is especially evident in the unanticipated results of the massive boycotts that gripped the racially separate universities of Fort Hare, University of the Western Cape (UWC), and the University of Durban-Westville in the early 1970s. Specifically, these struggles suggested that a tactical approach to boycott without a necessary critique of disciplinary reason would intensify the racialised grip over the subject. Let me draw briefly on the example of the 1973 student uprisings at UWC that were sparked by a comment made by a biochemist to a philosophy professor. The biochemist quoted Mao Tse Tung with a minor qualification. 'Power', he said, 'flowed from the barrel of the gun', and, he added, 'in this country whites have the guns'.[7] The students took exception to the comment. In the explosive events that followed, several student leaders were expelled from UWC. The rest of the story is anything but predictable. The state convened a commission of enquiry, which upon hearing evidence, recommended that the university be repositioned as a racial university, but not through the force of instrumentality. Rather, apartheid would ensure that the university be produced as a racial formation through the disciplinary mechanism of research.

The commission drew on the writings of academics, particularly Richard van der Ross, the vice-chancellor designate of UWC, to hand over the university as an "own affairs" project, but in keeping with the very racial logic of the state. To this end they adopted the spirit of Ross's intervention to produce a new idea of the university. Four points from a lengthy report may be worth citing, partly because they reveal that which was unforeseen in the struggles waged by students in the 1970s:

1. As far as possible, and particularly in the social sciences, we must relate closely to programmes of community action so that the attention of our student may be directed to the realities of our society.

2. We must not evade research into problems of poverty. Our research in this area must aim to cast new light on the problems of housing, transport, health, the preschool year, crime, poor motivation and so on.

3. We should not promote research into such matters that denigrate our own people as shiftless or alcoholics, but rather determine how they may achieve better insight into their own lives and how the situation may be improved.

4. We should not avoid basic economic, political and constitutional problems, but should rather persistently seek solutions which will provide satisfaction, justice and human dignity.

If anything, the consequence of the boycott set in place a research agenda aimed at normalisation of the university in the aftermath of the groundswell. It was a resolution of a crisis that favoured a more subtle operation of disciplinary power, but one that would increasingly be aimed at keeping the subject of disciplinary reason in its place.

What was unforeseen in the struggles of the 1970s, was that the boycott would give rise to a form of the subjection of agency, mediated through the apparatus of discipline and underwriting a new contract between the university and the state.

## Conclusion

A few weeks before completing this chapter, while browsing a second-hand book-shop in Cape Town, I stumbled upon a South African Institute of Race Relations Survey from 1986. It contained a report on the meeting of the NECC in Durban, and confirmation that two activists had indeed been killed while preparing to receive us in Durban. I felt unsettled by our wager on the veracity of receiving the news of the killing. If there was any meaning for the untimely deaths, I felt relieved that the boycott was ended after that meeting in March 1986. That decision was not because the boycott was tactically incorrect as a political statement, but that without a supple-mentary critique of disciplinary reason, the subject of that boycott would merely be one that is kept in its place. In the final analysis, naming the movement of students as a schools boycott proved insufficient to understand the mobilisation of thousands of students who decided in 1985 to set to work on the very object upon which they seemed to be acting, namely schooling.

# Endnotes

1   See P. Lalu, The Trojan Horse and the Becoming Technical of the Human, in R. Truscott, M. van Bever Donker, G. Minkley and P. Lalu, (eds.), *Remains of the Social* (forthcoming).

2   B. Massumi, Micropolitics: Exploring ethico-aesthetics, *Inflexions: A Journal of Research-Creation*, 2009, Vol. 3, October, 7.

3   See as an example of the rerouting of the debates of the 1980s, A. Sitze, Between Study and Revolt: Further notes on emergency continued, South African Contemporary History and Humanities Seminar, University of the Western Cape, 12 August 2014. See also P. Lalu, The Trojan Horse and the Becoming Technical of the Human, in R. Truscott, M. van Bever Donker, G. Minkley and P. Lalu (eds.), *Remains of the Social* (forthcoming).

4   ASAC Collection, RIM-UWC Mayibuye Archives, University of the Western Cape.

5   W. James and M. Simons (eds.). *The Angry Divide: Social and economic history of the Western Cape*, Cape Town: David Philip Publishers, 1989.

6   John Higgins, The Scholar-Warrior versus the Children of Mao: Connor Cruise O'Brien in South Africa, in B. Robbins (ed.), *Intellectuals: Aesthetics, Politics, Academics*. Minneapolis: University of Minnesota Press, 1990.

7   See P. Lalu and N. Murray, *Becoming UWC: Reflections, pathways and the unmaking of apartheid's legacy*. Cape Town: CHR, 2012.

Premesh Lalu is currently the director of the Centre for Humanities Research at the University of the Western Cape (UWC) and deputy dean for Research and Post-graduate Studies in the Faculty of Arts at UWC. He has lectured internationally and locally in South Africa on a broad range of themes, including histories of colonialism and apartheid. He is the author of *The Deaths of Hintsa: Post-apartheid South Africa and the shape of recurring pasts* (HSRC Press, 2009), and has published widely on South African history and present.

CHAPTER 14

# FIGHTING FOR
# 'OUR LITTLE FREEDOMS'[1]

## The evolution of student and youth politics in
## Phomolong township, Free State[2]

PHINDILE KUNENE

P homolong township, situated six kilometres from the small town of Hennenman
in the Free State, has received increased scholarly interest following its experience of service delivery protests in 2005.[3] Similarly, there has been a great
deal of interest in young political mobilisation and collective action under apartheid.[4]
Particularly intriguing is the belated development of youth political mobilisation in
the Free State and the varying reasons for this. It is argued here that the genesis of
youth political organising in Phomolong can only be understood against the backdrop
of the expansion of secondary schooling in the 1970s and 1980s. The permanent
presence of a young generation of students at high school level was absent in this area
until the late 1970s. In this absence of networks with established organisations, the
"locality" became a critical space for politicisation. Far from being an easy exercise,
challenging the powers of local authorities was a complex and contradictory process.
The kinship-like relations with councillors, their entrenched presence in the area as
revered "elders" and their location in the teaching profession meant that most of those
who later opposed them had actually benefited from their tutelage at one point or
another. Finally, the chapter argues that the emergence of a vigilante group – *Bontate*
(the fathers) – comprised almost exclusively of fathers and older male relatives of
the young activists confirms that youth political activity took a noticeable shape in
the latter part of the 1980s.

Seekings and Twala[5] pin the belated formation of youth political structures in the Free
State on a number of realities including the population size of some of its townships at

the time (only four townships boasted a population of more than 20 000 people), the relative isolation and disparate location of these townships with respect to one another, as well as their distance from urban areas that displayed decisive political mobilisation, particularly Johannesburg. Equally emphasised in the literature is the absence of educational institutions in the province that could be compared to Turfloop and Fort Hare as 'incubators of organised dissent'.[6] Unlike the relatively industrialised north-western part of the area, which is close to industrial centres like Sasolburg and boasts considerable strength in trade union organisation, the possibilities for political mobilisation in the southern Free State were limited by its overwhelmingly agricultural orientation. It is not surprising then that the first major instances of protest erupted in the north-western parts of the province, specifically, Tumahole township in Parys in 1985.

What is true for Phomolong, as it was for many parts of the country, is that the education reforms introduced from the 1970s meant that by the 1980s, secondary education had expanded significantly in African townships.[7] Until then, students from Phomolong could only access secondary schooling in neighbouring towns like Welkom and Kroonstad. The implication was that the township lacked a permanent presence of, and daily interface with, students at secondary school levels. Under these conditions, opportunities for the formation of formidable student organisations were stifled. Along with the expansion of secondary schooling, factors such as increased classroom overcrowding and excessive use of corporal punishment by teachers contributed to students acquiring a "generational consciousness" defined by demographic semblance and common suffering.[8] Bahale Secondary School, established in 1978, became the focal point of the emergence of this new awareness and crystallisation of contentious politics.

Seven years after the establishment of Bahale Secondary School in Phomolong, students began to organise on a noticeable scale. In early 1985, townships like Khotsong, Meloding Maokeng and Monyakeng – all neighbouring Phomolong – were experiencing a groundswell of political riots.[9] Phomolong was not left unscathed by the increased tempo of student protests in these areas. In August 1985, Phomolong experienced its first student protest at Bahale when a group composed predominantly of male students took on the case of the alleged sexual harassment of female students by the principal, Mr Ntwanyane Molapo. For Mile Fingers, a prominent activist, this was a formative experience:

[Many pupils] first saw politics in the name of the school principal who was sexually abusing female students. When he had sex with one of my classmates we decided to unite and take the issue up with the school board and the class monitors. We discovered that this man was still continuing ... in defiance when we would be requested to sing in the school assembly, we would sing 'Extra strong, Wilson extra strong'.[10]

Choosing what was then a popular advertising jingle for a famous brand of sweets as a protest song reflected the lack of politicisation among students at this time. More poignantly, it gave a clear indication that links with formal political organisations had not yet been established. As a further indication of political inexperience, the students placed their complaints about the principal's conduct on the doorstep of the class monitors and the school board. But things were about to change. Although the board was initially receptive to the students' concerns and assured them that 'they would try and counsel him [the principal] and show him that what he was doing is not right',[11] it became clear that it was not the first time that the board had heard about the principal's conduct, and this led to students taking matters into their own hands and threatening the principal with violence.

The school board reacted to the growing anger among students by suspending the principal and permitting democratic elections for a representative body of students, known as the "Big Ten". This new structure consisted exclusively of male students and included Thabo Sethunya, Tshidiso Mokati, Lehlohonolo Motingoe, Moshanyana Rathaba, Arrow Daliwe, Kgaki Matshai and Binkie Motsau, all of who became leading activists in the area.[12] Confident that it had regained control of the school, the board made the grave error of allowing the principal to return to the school. Students immediately disrupted classes, resulting in the school's closure for most of August 1985. The Department of Education and Training reacted by expelling the key leaders of the protests, who they labelled "boramerusu" – the agitators.[13] The response by education authorities to a campaign that students regarded as both legitimate and not explicitly political marked a turning point in the evolving political awareness of the students of Phomolong. No longer would they trust the authorities. Thus the campaign against sexual harassment also signalled the birth of student politics in the township.

The disruption of schooling in Bahale led to the members of the Big Ten being pursued by the South African Police (SAP). Suspended from school and needing to evade police arrest, some students relocated to neighbouring towns like Welkom and Kroonstad where nascent links with Black Consciousness-inspired activists existed. It was not until the detention of four members of the Big Ten in 1986, however, that traceable links with national movements emerged. One of the activists the Big Ten encountered in prison was Pat Matosa – an influential figure in Free State politics at the time. According to Thabo Sethunya, Matosa imparted lessons on history, resistance, the politics of black squatter movements and the meaning of the Soweto Uprising. He is also credited with teaching the young activists "freedom" songs and introducing them to historical figures like Sofasonke Mpanza. In this way, the detention of the Big Ten was a critical moment for young activists in Phomolong. Sello Sefuthi recalls:

> You know Hennenman is a small town, a small *dorpie*. I think it was
> a watershed moment when they came back from jail in 1986. To say,
> 'hey comrades, you must know that your other comrades somewhere in
> Soweto, wherever are in jails all over the country because of the same
> issues'.[14]

Although this is an important statement that captures the evolution of youth politics during this time, its significance should not be exaggerated since the detention period itself was no longer than twelve days. Nonetheless, these activists now saw themselves as a part of a broader movement and on their way to being integrated into national formations, which broke the isolation they had experienced in the small town.

## The formation of Phomolong Youth Congress (PYCO)

Following the example of their counterparts nationally, youth activists launched the Phomolong Youth Congress (PYCO) in February 1986. From its inception, PYCO concerned itself with youth matters such as unemployment, the lack of sports and recreational facilities, and teenage pregnancy. Organisers of the launch invited the mayor of the township, Mr Tsiane, which shows that they were not aware of the wide-spread rejection of black local authorities across the country. Instead, they imagined their interests in developing the township were shared by the mayor and his council:

> We explained to him what our vision was and he agreed with us. He
> agreed that we should advise them [the council] on issues regarding
> community development, youth development in particular.[15]

Mr Jacobs, a History teacher, became PYCO's first president, with Thabo Sethunya as chairperson and Kgaki Matshai as secretary. Mr Jacobs played a vital role in the early days of PYCO. Having graduated from Fort Hare, he proved to be an important source of political knowledge for the students. As a History teacher, he enjoyed the respect and affection of many of his students.[16] Despite the generally moderate stance of the organisers of the launch, the security police arrested key leaders on that first night, indicating the state's nervousness about the proliferation of political mobilisation among black youth across the province. The detention of youth activists participating in the PYCO launch is testimony to the fact that the Free State had come under strict surveillance during this time. A curfew was imposed on 11 magisterial districts in the Free State in June 1986[17] and when the state of emergency was declared more than 400 activists from the province were detained.[18]

Although parents were initially critical of PYCO's political activities, their attitudes shifted when the organisation started campaigning against the payment of housing rents, overcrowding, as well as the persistence of the bucket system of sewage removal. The rent increase issue, in particular, was one where PYCO received resounding support from older residents. In 1987, PYCO advanced a case that rents were too expensive for most residents to pay. They argued that residents in the older part of the township – Putswastene – were entitled to home ownership based on their prolonged occupation of those houses. Benjamin Litabe, a councillor and primary school teacher at the time, describes PYCO's tactics as follows:

> When rents would increase they would ... hit us. They didn't want rent
> increases. We suffered, it was painful, the youth did not want to hear
> anything. They said we are eating with the whites! They harassed us until
> we got out! They removed us![19]

PYCO called on the council to allocate sites on which residents could build houses to alleviate overcrowding, and also mobilised against the bucket system. For these young activists, the lack of proper sanitation was a curse inherited from one generation to the next:

> We come far with the bucket system. When my mother came to
> Phomolong with her mother from Marantha [old location] she found the
> bucket system in place. I was born with the bucket system still being
> used.[20]

Mobilising against black local authorities was far from easy. Councillors were revered by most of the members of the community. There were teachers, school principals, businessmen and church elders among them, whose social status earned them admiration and respect. Adult residents counted on councillors to resolve marital disputes and family feuds. At school level, young activists had passed through the tutelage of many teachers who simultaneously occupied roles as councillors in the apartheid local government edifice. This explains why PYCO's approach to councillors was either accommodating or hostile at various points in time. These nuances have also been highlighted in other studies.[21]

The sacred space that councillors occupied in the hearts of adult residents became evident when, in 1986, just after the release of the young activists, older men in the area, most of whom were related to the young activists, organised themselves into a grouping that would be known as *Bontate* – the fathers. Curiously, this group consisted of municipal police, councillors, prison warders, conservative church elders, businessmen and members of the school board, in other words, all the social forces that had an interest in the apartheid machinery. *Bontate* imposed a curfew in the area and inspected all the outside visitors who frequented the township. According to the young activists, *Bontate* would patrol the township and mete out physical punishment and discipline to any young person found roaming the streets after eight o'clock in the evenings. The formation of this grouping and its resorting to such harsh tactics against the young activists is demonstrable proof that youth political organising had assumed a noticeable form during this period.

## The Students' Congress

The expulsion of the Big Ten led to many challenges and a momentary lull in terms of student activism in Bahale. It also denied the students an organisational expression within the school. However, a new breed of radical students was beginning to organise in the school and they formed a branch of the Congress of South African Students (COSAS) in 1988.[22] The launch was celebratory and lasted the entire day with students reciting poems, singing and performing drama.[23] Students wore ANC colours, reflecting the growing dominance of the Congress movement among young activists. Members of the Students' Congress came mainly from Bahale and among the leaders were Sello Sefuthi, Banks Tshabangu, "Muthi" Musutu and Theo Masemola.

The organisation adopted the Freedom Charter and enjoyed some connections with national organisations. However, its campaigns remained firmly focused on local issues for the most part. Foremost among these was the demand for school authorities to permit students to leave the school premises during lunch break and have their lunch at home. The closure of the school gates during lunchtime was seen as disadvantaging poor students whose families could not pack them "proper" lunchboxes and therefore, granting students permission to leave the school during lunchtime would give them the opportunity to enjoy whatever provision was made for them in their homes without parading their poverty. The Students' Congress also took up campaigns on behalf of female students, especially those related to aesthetics and dress code. Students lamented that, 'girls couldn't have fancy hairstyles, as part of the apartheid laws. Women were not supposed to wear this and that'.[24] Taking up this type of issue was crucial in winning the support of female students.

Interestingly, the Students' Congress also championed language-related issues. An anti-Afrikaans campaign involving the burning of Afrikaans textbooks and literature within the school premises was attempted. To execute the campaign, students were encouraged to submit these texts which would be torched at the school's assembly point. The call received widespread support with students from most standards submitting their textbooks to form a heap in the assembly. However, while the call received substantial support from the students, the burning of the books did not proceed as planned:

The plan was to burn them in daylight when everyone was there. We couldn't go through with it. After about three days they started collecting their books. It was a question of who is going to burn them.[25]

The failure to burn the textbooks was attributed to the leadership's timidity. Parents who opposed the campaign did not make matters easy. Mosele Mahlatsi's sentiments about the campaign were expressed to her son in this fashion:

[Y]ou say you don't want Afrikaans but when I look at your results you have passed Afrikaans better than English and you are more fluent in Afrikaans than English. You are just going with the mob which doesn't want Afrikaans ... just look at how good you are in Afrikaans.[26]

Retrospectively, the leadership conceded that the campaign was ill-conceived and had the potential to lead to student failure.[27] Of course, they drew inspiration from the 1976 student uprising and continued to see Afrikaans as the language of the oppressor. At the same time, they encountered the different views expressed by their parents, who were also their allies in the broader struggle.

In 1989, the student and youth struggles took a dramatic turn by embracing violence, triggered by the alleged ritual killing of a young boy by a prominent local businessman. The ensuing combined action by the two formations occurred because of the strong overlap in the membership of their executives. According to Sefuthi and Musuthu, PYCO and Students' Congress leaders were approached by individual community members, who pleaded with them to "sort out" the perpetrator. They enthusiastically took up this campaign because the alleged perpetrator was also connected with key figures in the local council which targeted political activists in both formations. It was an opportunity to strike a blow against "the system". According to Musuthu, the young activists did not waste any time in taking up the call and viewed this as a critical moment in the struggle against the system of apartheid.

PYCO and the Students' Congress obtained the resources to undertake this campaign from the bereaved family. The activists sought money for petrol and set in motion a campaign that saw massive destruction of the businessman's property, including his house and shops.[28] In the late afternoon, the youth activists gathered at the entrance of the township and started singing, brandishing the makeshift petrol bombs.[29] Other members of the community later joined them in numbers. The amount of support received surprised some members of PYCO. As one of the activists relates: 'When we started singing we were about nine or ten around four o'clock but by the time it was six o'clock the whole township was there!'[30]

Although the campaign fulfilled its immediate task, which was to destroy the perpetrator's properties and business, there were also serious ramifications for this action both at an individual activist level and more broadly at the organisational level. Henceforth, violence would play a crucial role in defining political contestation, which reframed relations between the student/youth movements and the authorities, as well as with parents, and affected the character of the movements.

## Conclusion

The first form of noticeable student political organising in Phomolong coincided with the expansion of secondary schooling across the country in the 1980s. It has been argued here that the establishment of the township's first high school contributed to the development of a layer of politicised youth and also acted as a convenient site for youth political activity. The tale of PYCO attests to the notion that although repression stifled political mobilisation, it also aided it by bringing activists into contact and broadening their horizon beyond their immediate areas. Protesting apartheid structures within and outside the schooling environment was not as clear-cut as many would like to believe. As has been argued in this paper, young activists shared an ambivalent relationship with councillors and school authorities. The social status and the kinship relations that councillors and representatives in the school board had with young activists complicated matters in ways that this article has only briefly articulated.

# Endnotes

1   Interview with M. Musutu (student activist) by Phindile Kunene, Phomolong, 17 September 2009

2   This chapter draws substantially from research done for my unpublished MA dissertation, From Apartheid to Democracy: A historical analysis of local struggles in Phomolong Township, Free State. University of the Witwatersrand, 2011.

3   See LJS. Botes et al, *The New Struggle: Service delivery-related unrest in South Africa*, Centre for Development Support, University of Free State, 2007; and P. Kunene, From Apartheid to Democracy: A historical analysis of local struggles in Phomolong Township, Free State: 1985–2005, MA dissertation, University of the Witwatersrand, 2013.

4   See C. Glaser, Youth Culture and Politics in Soweto, 1958–1976, PhD Thesis, Cambridge University, 1994; A. Sitas, The Making of the Comrades' Movement in Natal: 1985–91, *Journal of Southern African Studies*, 1992, 18(3), 629-41; C. Carter, Comrades and Community: Politics and the construction of hegemony in Alexandra Township, South Africa, 1984–1987, PhD thesis, University of Oxford, 1991; J. Seekings, *Heroes or Villains? Youth politics in the 1980s*, Johannesburg: Ravan Press, 1993; M. Marks, Organisations, Identity and Violence amongst Activist Diepkloof Youth: 1984–1993, MA dissertation, University of the Witwatersrand, 1993; MS. Ndlovu, The Soweto Uprising: Part 1, in South African Democracy Education Trust (SADET) (ed.). *The Road to Democracy in South Africa, Volume 2 (1970–1980)*. Pretoria: UNISA Press, 2006.

5   C. Twala and J. Seekings, Activist Networks and Political Protest in the Free State, 1983–1990, in South African Democracy Education Trust (SADET) (ed.). *The Road to Democracy in South Africa, Vol. 4, 1980–1990*. Pretoria: UNISA Press, 2010, 788-9.

6   Ibid, 767.

7   Ibid, 169.

8   C. Bundy, Street Sociology and Pavement Politics: Aspects of youth and student resistance in Cape Town, 1985, *Journal of Southern African Studies*, 1987, 13(3), April, 316.

9   C. Twala and J. Seekings, Activist Networks and Political Protest in the Free State, 1983–1990, 788-9.

10  Interview with M. Fingers (former PYCO/student activist) by Phindile Kunene (Local Histories, Present Realities Collection), Wits University, Phomolong, 19 September 2009.

11  Ibid.

12  Ibid.

13  Interview with S. Sethunya (former PYCO/student activist) by Phindile Kunene (Local Histories, Present Realities Collection), Wits University, Phomolong, 05 March 2009.

14  Interview with S. Sethunya (former PYCO/student activist) by Phindile Kunene (Local Histories, Present Realities Collection), Wits University, Welkom, 27 November 2009.

15  Interview with S. Sethunya (former PYCO/student activist), 05 March 2009.

16  Jacobs left Phomolong shortly after the arrests and was never seen again.

17  C. Twala and J. Seekings, Activist Networks and Political Protest in the Free State, 1983–1990, 802.

18  D. Webster, Repression and the State of Emergency, *South African Review*, 1987, Vol. 4. Johannesburg: Ravan Press, 151.

19  Interview with B. Litabe (former councillor) by Phindile Kunene (Local Histories, Present Realities Collection), Wits University, Phomolong, 24 July 2009.

20  Interview with M. Musutu (student activist), 17 September 2009.

21  T. Moloi, Black Politics in Kroonstad: Political mobilisation, protests, local government, and generational struggles, 1976–1995. Unpublished PhD thesis, University of the Witwatersrand, 2012.

22  Although COSAS was banned in 1985, many of the interviewees insist that they launched a body by this name in 1988. Because of the lack of clarity on this question, I refer to this body as the Students' Congress rather than COSAS.

23  Interview with M. Musutu (student activist), 17 September 2009.

24  Interview with S. Sefuthi (former PYCO activist/student activist), 27 November 2009.

25  Interview with M. Musutu (student activist), 17 September 2009.

26  Interview with M. Mahlatsi (parent) by Phindile Kunene (Local Histories, Present Realities Collection), Wits University, Phomolong, 20 September 2009.

27  Interview with M. Musutu (student activist), 17 September 2009.

28  When I started doing the interviews in 2009, the alleged perpetrator's house remained in its burnt state. There was also no occupancy in this burnt house.

29  Interview with M. Musutu (student activist), 17 September 2009; and interview with S. Sefuthi (former PYCO activist/student activist), 27 November 2009.

30  Interview with M. Musutu (student activist), 17 September 2009.

Phindile Kunene holds an MA in History (University of the Witwatersrand). Her research variously explored the history of the local state in South Africa, youth political activism, apartheid forms of co-option and youth political demobilisation. She has also explored post-apartheid forms and repertoires of collective action and protest. An activist herself, she has been involved in youth and student movements and trade unions, and currently works as an educator and curriculum specialist servicing activist organisations.

CHAPTER 15

# 'EVERY GENERATION HAS ITS STRUGGLE'[1]

## A brief history of Equal Education (2008–15)

BRAD BROCKMAN

E qual Education (EE) is a movement of high school students, parents, teachers and community members campaigning for quality and equality in the South African education system. Established in 2008 in Khayelitsha in the Western Cape, EE was the idea of veteran activist Zackie Achmat, co-founder of the Treatment Action Campaign (TAC). EE is a membership-based movement that organises high school students in branches across the country, and uses research, social mobilisation and the law to ensure that students' constitutional right to education is realised and the legacy of colonial and apartheid education undone.

EE's first organisers and leaders were UCT law graduates Doron Isaacs and Yoliswa Dwane, who started working full-time for what was then called the Applied Education Research Organisation (AERO) on 1 February 2008. Achmat had called the first meeting of AERO at his home in Muizenberg, Cape Town on 14 December 2006,[2] and had two researchers start summarising education research. Isaacs and Dwane recruited a team of organisers – Lumkile Zani, Lwandiso Stofile, Nokubonga Yawa and Joey Hasson – and set up a small office in the SHAWCO Centre in Khayelitsha.

Together, the group spent the initial months sitting in classrooms in Khayelitsha, observing and learning, and coming together in the afternoon to discuss what they had seen and to run seminars for themselves. The group also drew on the experience of members of the EE Board, including Achmat and Professor Mary Metcalfe, the ANC's first MEC for Education in Gauteng, as well as other important advisors like Professor Paula Ensor, then head of the School of Education at UCT, Professor Crain Soudien and Advocate Rob Peterson.

EE was modelled on the TAC, which, since its founding in 2008, had successfully campaigned for a public antiretroviral treatment programme, doing battle with a government led by an AIDS denialist, former President Thabo Mbeki, and super-profiting drug companies. The TAC had developed an approach to struggle which EE would emulate, grounding its claims in the rights contained in the Constitution, while basing its power in a politicised, informed and organised mass membership.

Like the TAC, EE is politically independent, though as Isaacs, EE's first coordinator, explains, being based in working-class communities shapes EE's politics:

> In articulating a fresh politics EE was not loyal to the ANC, to the organisations whose flags flew at the front of the liberation struggle in South Africa. But we always orientated towards those organisations, because that's where the mass of the people were – and to a diminished extent still are – where they placed their hopes and felt their unity and strength. We took that very seriously, and orientated ourselves towards them.[3]

## Youth Group

The organisers decided to arrange a first meeting of high school youth from Khayelitsha on 24 April 2008. By then the organisation had been renamed Equal Education. They advertised the meeting by handing out flyers and inviting students they had met. Hasson, who led EE's youth organising work, remembers catering for 40. Yet only seven students showed up. But he says, 'every meeting grew from that moment onwards largely by word of mouth. People spoke to their friends. People talked on the street ... there was an exponential growth'.[4]

This space that brings EE members together on a weekly basis was named Youth Group, and remains the primary method by which EE's high school student members – who started calling themselves "equalisers" in 2008 – are organised. Equalisers attend a structured weekly Youth Group meeting run by a facilitator, most often a former equaliser. There they meet students from other schools; learn about history, politics and activism; discuss issues in their homes, schools and communities; and plan and discuss EE campaigns.

Pharie Sefali, who joined EE in Grade 11, and today works in its head office as a political materials developer, remembers Youth Group as 'a safe space' where equalisers 'could talk about issues we don't normally talk about at home or at school, and not feel judged'. She remembers playing games and how when they sang at Youth Group 'it gave us a sense of unity and being part of the same struggle'. 'We used to read a lot,' she contunues, 'we learned about our rights and the constitution, and how people in South Africa and other countries organised to beat oppressive systems and achieve a common goal'.[5]

Ntsiki Dlulani, who joined EE in 2009 when EE expanded beyond Khayelitsha, says '[w]e saw Equal Education as a platform for us young people to express ourselves and how we feel about the education system'. Dlulani remembers being able to identify with the issues raised by other students: 'We had students from Khayelitsha telling us that they're facing inside their schools not having a library, a field, a qualified teacher … windows are broken and roofs are falling … So we were like, oh, that's the same thing we are facing'.[6]

The model for Youth Group came from Habonim Dror, a Jewish youth movement which Isaacs and Hasson had previously led, and from which a number of the first heads of EE Youth Group were drawn. By 2011, youth groups were headed by former equalisers who had graduated from high school in Khayelitsha and other townships where EE was organised. Today there are more than 3 000 equalisers from over 100 schools attending weekly youth groups run by 150 trained facilitators in the Western Cape, Gauteng, the Eastern Cape, KwaZulu-Natal and Limpopo.

## Early campaigns: Broken Windows (2008) and Late Coming (2009)

EE's first campaign originated in a series of youth group activities on the power of photography and film. Equalisers were given disposable cameras and asked to take photographs of what they felt prevented them from receiving a quality education. One of the photographs, taken by Zukiswa Vuka, was of a wall of broken windows at her school, Luhlaza High in Khayelitsha. EE's first campaign was to have the more than 500 broken windows at Luhlaza fixed.

EE met with the school principal, teachers and students at the school, as well as with officials in the Western Cape Education Department (WCED). The school said that it had been asking for years for the windows to be fixed, while the WCED claimed that it was unaware of the problem. A petition calling on the WCED to fix the windows and committing students to look after them was signed by more than 2 000 supporters of the campaign through a door-to-door sign-on effort in Khayelitsha.

Some WCED officials actively sought to obstruct the campaign, telling principals not to work with EE and trying to intimidate students participating in the campaign. These officials, assisted by local SADTU members and the Khayelitsha Education Forum (KEF), were threatened by organised and politicised students asserting themselves and drawing attention to the dismal state of education in the area. After an article[7] written by equalisers Phatiswa Shushwana and Lwando Mzandisi was published in the *Cape Times*, Robin Botes, a circuit team manager in Khayelitsha told Mzandisi that 'a black child from Khayelitsha is not able to write such an article'.

EE organised a rally of 450 students in central Cape Town on 10 October 2008. Before the rally, equalisers had written media articles; prepared poetry, placards and speeches; and mobilised other students – at the time, Youth Group had a membership of about 150 and many had been trained as spokespersons and marshals. At a public meeting in Khayelitsha on 13 November 2008, Western Cape Education MEC Yousuf Gabru commited to fixing the windows at Luhlaza and investing an additional R671 000 in the school. The windows were fixed that December holiday. This was EE's first campaign victory. It became a model for future EE campaigns, inspired confidence in members and drew new members to the movement, excited by what had been achieved at Luhlaza.

EE's next campaign, in early 2009, focused on the issue of late coming, which equalisers had identified as being a major problem in their schools. Academic research showed that 20% of students in South Africa arrived late for school each morning, and that 20% of teaching and learning time was lost each day due to late coming and absenteeism. The campaign was led by equalisers in their schools and directed at fellow students. An equaliser Leadership Committee, consisting of representatives from each school, was established to coordinate the campaign and this remains a feature of EE's youth organising work.

Ntuthuzo Ndzomo, elected deputy general secretary at EE's 2015 National Congress, was an equaliser in 2009 and participated in the campaign:

We had to actually wake up early, arrive at school early, speak to our teachers. I remember our principal used to make announcements about it. He was really into it because he liked the idea that learners were taking initiative of making sure that others learners were arriving at school on time. So when we would arrive at the school, he would be there. We would stand outside the school, distributing pamphlets, singing, with posters, with messages motivating other learners to arrive early.[8]

The campaign ran for three weeks and visibly reduced the number of students arriving late at the schools where the campaign was run. At Ndzomo's school, Esangweni High, the number of students arriving late went from 121 at the beginning of the campaign to just one by the end of it.

## National campaigns: Libraries (2009–11) and Norms and Standards for School Infrastructure (2011–13)

EE's first national campaign aimed to address the low levels of literacy and lack of access to books at most South African schools. Only 7% of schools in the country had stocked and functioning libraries. In working-class communities like Khayelitsha, where there are also few public libraries, young people face a critical lack of books for reading and research. As Abongile Ndesi, one of the more than 3 000 students who attended EE's march for school libraries on 22 September 2009 told a journalist, '[w]e want more information and knowledge'.[9]

A few months earlier, on 4 and 5 July 2009, around 70 EE activists, mostly high school students, had gathered in Franschhoek, Western Cape, for an intense weekend. They spent it together reading academic research into the school library question and formulating the strategy and tactics of what would be EE's first campaign to speak directly to national government policy.

EE demanded that the Department of Basic Education (DBE) adopt a policy and a plan to provide every school in South Africa with a library and a librarian. The campaign's slogan was "1 School. 1 Library. 1 Librarian". The organisation wrote letters to the minister, lobbied government officials and parliamentarians, fasted for 24 hours and picketed the Publishers' Association of South Africa conference to protest the high cost of books. EE produced a sizeable booklet on the relationship between access to books and academic achievement, which included a detailed costing plan for providing libraries across the country.

On 21 March 2010, equalisers marched to Parliament in Cape Town, following a concert with performers HHP and Simphiwe Dana and speeches by Congress of South African Trade Unions (COSATU) General Secretary Zwelinzima Vavi and Young Communist League (YCL) President Buti Manamela. There were also smaller marches in Pretoria and Polokwane. The movement had moved beyond its Western Cape beginnings.

Professor Njabulo Ndebele and education analyst Graeme Bloch attended the march in Cape Town. They wrote an article for the *Sunday Times*, which began:

> On Human Rights Day, March 21, a Sunday, 10 000 high school pupils marched through the centre of Cape Town in school uniform. They were children, predominantly of working class origins, from all over the Western Cape, rural and urban, black and white. Not a rock or a bottle was thrown as they dispersed peacefully to the trains that had been arranged to take them home.

> The children were marching for books. In 2010, when we have built nine football stadiums across the country and will undoubtedly run an organised and inspiring World Cup, children were marching under the same banner as 1976: Equal Education.[10]

In a letter responding to EE's memorandum of 21 March 2010, minister of Basic Education Angie Motshekga wrote that she was about to adopt the National Policy for an Equitable Provision of an Enabling School Physical Teaching and Learning Environment (NPEP). 'This policy,' she wrote, 'will be followed by the Norms and Standards for School Infrastructure, in terms of which all schools will have a central-ised library'. It was the first time EE had heard about the norms and standards.

EE's organisers found a comprehensive 2008 draft, issued under the previous minister of Education, Naledi Pandor. The basis of the norms and standards was Section 5A of the South African (SASA) Schools Act of 1996: 'The minister may, after consultation with the minister of Finance and the Council of Education ministers, by regulation prescribe uniform norms and standards for school infrastructure'. It went on to define what services and physical infrastructure were to be included.

The NPEP was adopted in June 2010 and binding norms and standards were meant to follow by the end of March 2011. The leadership of EE saw this as an opportunity. The norms and standards would be regulations rather than policy and therefore would be legally binding. They would address all school infrastructure backlogs, from electricity and water to school libraries, and the minister had committed to adopting them. It was decided then to broaden the libraries campaign into a campaign for norms and standards for school infrastructure.

A large march was planned for 21 March 2011, as a reminder to Minister Motshekga to keep her promise and also to raise public awareness. Organisers and equalisers mobilised students at schools across the Western Cape, and DJ Oskido and musicians Freshly Ground performed at a concert preceding the march. South African Democratic Teachers' Union (SADTU) General Secretary Mugwena Maluleke addressed the march, and by the time that equaliser Unathi Mnani took to the stage, 20 000 students stood before her on Cape Town's Grand Parade. Mnani told them:

> Today we demand "Minimum Norms and Standards for School Infrastructure". These norms and standards will say that every school must have electricity, water, safe buildings, enough toilets, a staffroom and other facilities. The minister must finalise these norms and standards in the next ten days. That is our demand. After that, communities can campaign to get schools fixed to those standards.[11]

The minister did not adopt norms and standards at the end of March 2011. In all, throughout the libraries and school infrastructure campaigns, likely over 150 000 people signed petitions, over one million leaflets were handed out at train stations and taxi ranks, over 50 000 individuals participated in marches, and the number of media reports ran into the hundreds if not thousands. But it would take Motshekga more than two-and-a-half years, legal proceedings prepared by the Legal Resources

Centre, two settlement agreements, two draft policies, a 48-hour occupation outside Parliament and repeated mass marches across the country, before she eventually adopted binding norms and standards in November 2013.

## Parent organising

At the beginning of 2011, EE began establishing parent branches in Khayelitsha. It saw organised parent support as vital to strengthening its position within schools and communities, as well as in campaign work. By then it had been organising students for three years, and assumed it could convert this experience into organising parents. This proved more difficult than anticipated. Initial ideas of when, how long and what the content of parent branch meetings should be were all revised through a slow process of trial and error.

By the middle of 2012, three parent branches had been established, each with its own executive elected by branch members. A campaign was run to raise the profile of the school governing body elections, and to get EE parents elected. And parents were becoming involved in EE's wider campaigning activity. By the middle of 2013, EE had nine active parent branches in the Western Cape, and the beginnings of parent organising in Gauteng.

## Equal Education Law Centre

Dedicated legal support for both long-term campaigns and reactive mobilisation was felt increasingly necessary. Therefore at the beginning of 2012, the Equal Education Law Centre (EELC) was established as an independent organisation, with Dmitri Holtzman as executive director and former Chief Justice Arthur Chaskalson as chairperson of its Board. The EELC would act as EE's lawyers, collaborate with EE on research and policy work, and jointly formulate campaign and legal strategy with EE leaders. In addition, this partnership has attended almost every parliamentary portfolio committee meeting on education in the past five years, and made around a dozen submissions. The EELC continues today with Nurina Ally as executive director and Kate O'Regan as chairperson.

## Democratising EE: Congress 2012

From 8–11 July 2012, EE held its first elective National Congress at the University of Johannesburg. This was a key moment in the history of EE and marked the organisation's transition from an NGO to an internally-democratic movement, in which members participated actively in decision-making and felt a sense of ownership of the organisation. The push towards Congress was also motivated by the then leadership's desire to cement the movement's popular legitimacy in two ways: by demonstrating the democratic control of its mass base, and by electing a predominantly black leadership, which was achieved.

Hundreds of student, parent, post-school youth and staff delegates, representing branches mainly from the Western Cape, but also from Gauteng, the Eastern Cape, KwaZulu-Natal and Limpopo, attended Congress. Delegates elected the movement's leadership – a representative National Council to replace the Board – adopted a new constitution, and decided on a set of resolutions which would guide the movement until the next Congress three years later. These resolutions emphasised the need to grow the movement nationally, build wider support for EE's work, and win campaigns, particularly the campaign for norms and standards.

Yoliswa Dwane was elected as chairperson, Brad Brockman as general secretary, Doron Isaacs as deputy general secretary, Ntuthuzo Ndzomo as deputy chairperson (post-school youth representative), Bayanda Mazwi as deputy chairperson (equaliser representative) and Sean Feinberg as treasurer.

## National expansion

One of the resolutions adopted at the 2012 Congress was to grow the movement nationally. EE began to dedicate full-time resources to supporting members in provinces without an office and employed staff in Limpopo, KwaZulu-Natal and the Eastern Cape. Facilitators were trained, material was sent and support provided so that youth groups and campaigns could take place in these provinces.

EE had opened an office in Tembisa, Gauteng, in early 2012. However it was not until the middle of 2013, when Tshepo Motsepe and Adam Bradlow became co-heads, that work in Gauteng got off the ground. A provincial sanitation campaign started in August 2013 with equalisers doing a two-week sanitation audit of 11 of the 13 high schools in

Tembisa. The audit found that in over half the schools more than 100 students had to share a single working toilet.

At the beginning of 2014, then Gauteng Education MEC Barbara Creecy responded by having two pre-fabricated toilet blocks delivered to five schools in Tembisa. However, these toilets were to remain locked for the next six months, despite EE's appeals to the MEC, because the toilets had not been installed properly and principals were not confident the toilets would ever be replaced by permanent structures. With the general elections approaching, the campaign was broadened to include Daveyton and KwaThema where equalisers faced similar conditions in their schools.

Following the general elections, Panyaza Lesufi was appointed as the new MEC in June. In response to an EE march to his office on 11 September, Lesufi announced that he would allocate R150 million to fix the toilets at 580 schools in the province. This was a major victory, which directly affected the schooling of more than 600 000 working-class students in Gauteng. It was followed up by a social audit of more than 200 schools in 20 working-class communities. More than 500 volunteers from EE, civic and religious organisations and community-based structures participated in the audit. At a summit held in May 2015 to announce the results of the audit, MEC Lesufi accepted all EE's demands and committed a further R50 million to improving school infrastructure in the province.

EE opened its third office in October 2014 in King William's Town in the Eastern Cape. The office was to serve as a base for organising rural students, parents, and teachers to monitor the implementation of the norms and standards for school infrastructure in their schools. EE had made a strategic decision to focus this work on the Eastern Cape, while continuing to monitor the budgets and expenditure, progress reports and parliamentary submissions of the DBE and provincial education departments.

In Nquthu in KwaZulu-Natal (KZN), where students walk up to 24 kilometres a day to get to and from school, equalisers have been campaigning for scholar transport since 2014. On 9 April 2015, 500 equalisers marched to the KZN Department of Education offices in Pietermartizburg, demanding transport for the schools in Nquthu, full implementation of the existing KZN scholar transport policy and the adoption of a national scholar transport policy and a conditional grant to fund its implementation.

## Congress 2015

From 4–8 July 2015 EE held its second elective Congress at the University of the Western Cape. Delegates to Congress represented the movement's more than 3 000 equalisers, 100 facilitators, 13 parent branches and nearly 80 staff members. At the time of Congress, EE was actively campaigning for the implementation of norms and standards, school sanitation in Gauteng, scholar transport in KZN and safety and sanitation in Western Cape schools.

There was much for Congress to celebrate in terms of campaigns and national growth. However, it was clear that while the National Council and the Secretariat had met regularly over the previous three years, and made important strategic decisions, the structures had not functioned as well as hoped. Although these structures met regularly, and took decisions in line with EE's new constitution, the extent to which a vibrant, regularly consultative culture was realised fell short of expectations.

Congress resolved to continue with EE's current campaigns, as well as to develop and run a national campaign on learning and teaching over the next three years. Yoliswa Dwane was elected as chairperson, Tshepo Motsepe as general secretary, Ntuthuzo Ndzomo as deputy general secretary, Tracey Malawana as deputy chairperson (post-school youth representative), Buhle Booi as deputy chairperson (equaliser representative) and Doron Isaacs as treasurer.

## Conclusion

Over the past eight years, EE has evolved from a small NGO in the Western Cape to a mass movement, which is internally democratic and has thousands of high school students, post-school youth and parent members across the country. Political educa-tion is at the centre of youth groups and parent branches, and these structures form the basis of the movement's organising and campaign work. EE has run successful campaigns to fix broken windows, decrease late-coming, secure additional textbooks and teachers, establish school infrastructure standards, improve school sanitation and safety, and ensure the provision of scholar transport.

EE has raised considerable funds from international foundations, all of which have been disclosed in annually published financial statements. That reflects the high priority the organisation has placed on internal administration – largely the work of Michelle

Adler, Yoni Bass and Ntshadi Mofokeng. A number of former equalisers are now staff members, managers and part of the political leadership of EE, and there have been two successful elective Congresses held thus far. As the movement continues to grow, its challenge will be to continue delivering quality political education to members, to strengthen internal democracy, to continue winning campaigns for quality and equal education for all, and to connect its work with broader youth, worker and community struggles.

## Endnotes

1   "Every generation has its struggle" is an Equal Education slogan used on t-shirts and political materials.
2   The meeting was attended by Zackie Achmat, Andrew Warlick, Elaine Morris, Byron Morris, Mazibuko Jara, Nick Friedman, Dalli Weyers, Eduard Grebe and Jordan Goldwarg.
3   Doron Isaacs, electronic communication with author, 2 April 2016.
4   Interview with Joey Hasson by Jonathon Fairhead, Cape Town, 18 June 2015.
5   Pharie Sefali, electronic communication with author, 4 April 2016.
6   Interview with Ntsiki Dlulani by Jonathon Fairhead, Cape Town, 25 August 2015.
7   Phatiswa Shushwana and Lwando Mzandisi, Shattered glass, broken system, *Cape Times,* 8 October 2008. Interview with Ntuthuzo Ndzomo by Jonathon Fairhead, Cape Town, 24 August 2015.
8   Interview with Ntuthuzo Ndzomo by Jonathon Fairhead, Cape Town, 24 August 2015.
9   CW. Dugger, South African Children Push for Better Schools, *New York Times,* 24 September 2009.
10  G. Bloch, and NS. Ndebele, The New Struggle: One school, one library, one librarian, *Sunday Times,* 11 April 2010.
11  Equal Education Annual Report 2010 and 2011, 16.

Brad Brockman was the general secretary of Equal Education from 2012–15. Before then he worked at the organisation as a researcher and community organiser. Brockman has a BA degree in History and Politics and an Honours degree in History from UCT. He is currently an activist fellow with the Bertha Foundation and the Social Change Initiative, and is based in New York. Brockman remains a member of Equal Education's National Council.

# CHAPTER 16

# CONTEMPORARY STUDENT POLITICS IN SOUTH AFRICA

## The rise of the black-led student movements of #RhodesMustFall and #FeesMustFall in 2015

### LEIGH-ANN NAIDOO

The 2015 October student uprisings in South Africa, organised around the hashtag and demand that #FeesMustFall (also #EndOutsourcing and #NationalShutDown), have been compared to the student uprisings of June 1976 when thousands of youth took to the streets to protest against the apartheid government's insistence that Afrikaans be a compulsory medium of instruction in schools. While the June 1976 and the October 2015 student uprisings were organised around what can, on the surface, be understood as a single issue, these large-scale protests also wanted larger demands to be met. The students of 1976 were resisting the unequal and segregated school and societal system of apartheid and in 2015 students were resisting the commodification of education by calling for free, quality, decolonised education and expressing dissatisfaction with the rate and depth of change two decades after South Africa's democratisation. Youth were critiquing the institutional racism and the racialised oppression that have persisted across South Africa, making it arguably the most unequal country in the world currently.[1]

Comparing the recent 2015 uprisings to the 1968–69 period seems appropriate as that was the year that Steve Biko and others formed the South African Students' Organisation (SASO). Out of this radical black student organisation came the politics and philosophy of Black Consciousness (BC), which encouraged self-reflection and the centering of the black self, and insisted on a Pan-African outlook. In its early phases it critiqued the education system in South Africa and fought for the improvement of higher education for the black student. It also developed its own organisational practices and structures and a political education programme (known as Leadership Training programmes for university students and Formation Schools for high school students and community members) for its members. There was a significant change in thinking about education and society from 1969 onwards, when SASO stopped fighting for "equality" in education, or education equal to white education, and started criticising white, privileged education as a domesticating or dominating education.

The last few years have seen a re-emergence of BC and Pan-Africanism at universities through a range of student formations. The demographics of universities, particularly the historically-white institutions like the University of Cape Town (UCT), Rhodes University, University of Pretoria and University of Stellenbosch, have changed significantly since black students were allowed into all universities. At some universities this has meant that black students make up the majority of students on campus. Yet black students describe their experience of being on campus as alienating. Black students have recognised and discussed how the norm at universities continues to cater for white, middle class, heterosexual, able-bodied men, and how this institutionalised norm can be seen in the continued dominance of white, middle class, male professors who continue to hold the most power and influence at universities. Black students, as a result, have followed the BC tradition of becoming conscious of one's own condition and the conditions of other black people as the first step to changing those conditions. BC also insists that black people, once conscious, become their own liberators by first freeing their minds from the oppressions of a racist, capitalist, sexist and patriarchal world, and then working together to free themselves physically or change the material conditions of black students' lives. The black-led student movements that were formed in 2015 work with these guiding principles as a response to a university environment that continues to remain largely untransformed.

## Black students rise

The initial student movement activity of 2015 was thrust into the public imagination in March 2015 at UCT with the #RhodesMustFall (RMF) black-led student movement. Students at UCT centred their protest on – and named it for – the visible figure of the statue of imperialist Cecil John Rhodes, which sat in pride of place on the university's upper campus, but they also articulated a range of demands around inadequate transformation of the university's staff and its curricula, and barriers of access to the university for poor students. These issues spread and expanded throughout the year via the Black Students' Movement (BSM) at the university currently known as Rhodes, the October6 movement at the University of the Witwatersrand (Wits) and the University of Johannesburg (UJ), Open Stellenbosch (OS) at the University of Stellenbosch (US), the Black Student Stokvel at Nelson Mandela Metropolitan University (NMMU), and, more recently, via Transform Pukke at North West University (NWU), and UPrising at the University of Pretoria (UP). These institutionally-based black-led student movements were all organised around, and were thinking through, the decolonisation of their universities by opposing the colonial signs and symbols that remain on their campuses, and spoke out against institutional and interpersonal racism, in most cases, by calling for an end to the oppressive system of outsourcing.[2]

There were further protests at institutions throughout 2015 that dealt with a number of additional issues. These included insufficient residences to house students and the lack of access to them over holiday periods (at Rhodes University and the University of KwaZulu-Natal (UKZN)); the corruption and inadequacies of the National Student Financial Aid Scheme (NSFAS) at Fort Hare and the Tshwane University of Technology (TUT), among other institutions; the heritage symbols and institutional racism at North West University (NWU) and the University of the Free State (UFS); and the language policy and institutional racism at the University of Stellenbosch, to name a few. University students again captured the imagination of people across the country and abroad when a documentary film called *Luister* (Listen), where students give telling accounts of racism at the University of Stellenbosch, was circulated online.

Even though BC and Pan-Africanism are the rallying calls and political philosophy of the 2015 student movement, there is another key question and position foregrounded by RMF at UCT and followed in varying forms by other student movements. RMF identified three key pillars from the beginning of the movement: Black Consciousness, Pan-Africanism, and the concept of intersectionality. This meant that the movement acknowledged a number of oppressive systems in addition to racism and capitalism and was committed to trying to work against all oppressions that presented themselves in universities, and were also present within the student movements. The balancing act of BC, Pan-Africanism and intersectionality meant that there were more women and queer students voicing their concerns and participating more fully in the early stages of the movements. But as the student movements continued to struggle to decolonise their universities through an intersectional understanding of privilege and oppression, there was more and more resistance from a number of men in the movements who tried to argue that the issue of racism should trump all other issues. There was a shift from the October 2015 #FeesMustFall protests that placed class squarely on the struggle agenda, which resulted in movements centering race and class as the primary oppressive systems to fight against. Many students made the argument that the struggle needed to focus on one or two things and could not take on everything at once. Black queer feminists in the movement resisted this approach and continued to draw attention to the oppressive systems of patriarchy and homophobia, compelling their heterosexual male comrades to recognise that while they are oppressed as black men in a university system and world that continues to privilege whiteness, they are simultaneously privileged as men by patriarchy and by heteronormativity as heterosexual. This key issue has proven to be a challenge internal to most student movements and highlights the continued ideological and power struggles taking place.

By October 2015 these student movements were actively linking themselves to one another across the country. A national day of action to demand an end to outsourcing on 6 October was initiated by the October6 movement at Wits and UJ with RMF, BSM, and OS joining in to organise a national day of protest. This was followed by further national protests, and the shutdown of universities across the country from 14 October, demanding greater access to higher education through the issue of fees and financial exclusions under the banner #FeesMustFall.

The broader questions of the student movements mentioned above formed part of the overarching question of decolonisation, of both the university and South African society. The student movement programme of decolonisation differentiated itself from the programme of transformation driven by the African National Congress (ANC)-led government and its student organisations. Student movements critiqued the concept of transformation and exposed how the transformation agenda at universities seemed to be dealing with surface-level cosmetic changes. The movements called instead for deeper structural change of the university as an institution, issuing from concerns with staff demographics, Euro-centric curricula, institutional racism and other forms of oppression such as patriarchy and homophobia. The key thinkers being used by these movements included Frantz Fanon, Steve Biko, Ngugi Wa Thiong'o, Audre Lorde, Robert Sobukwe, bell hooks, Amilcar Cabral, and Kimberlé Crenshaw. These authors engage with ideas of Pan-Africanism, black self-empowerment, decolonisation, and intersectionality, among others.

## #Fees Must Fall (FMF)

The majority of the Student Representative Councils (SRCs) at universities have been dominated by the ANC-aligned Progressive Youth Alliance (PYA), consisting of the South African Students' Congress (SASCO), the ANC Youth League, the Young Communist League and the Muslim Students' Association. This has meant that the project of transformation remained the focus of ANC-led SRCs. Meanwhile, the broader student movements that were formed in 2015 and which were largely non-partisan, spoke out against the transformational agenda of the last 20-odd years as insufficient and superficial, and focused instead on imagining a programme of decolonisation.

The #FeesMustFall campaign started on 14 October 2015 at Wits University but it was quickly joined by the already-existing national conversations that had led to the #EndOutsourcing national day of action the week before. Students from Rhodes University called for the #NationalShutdown campaign, to intensify the FMF campaign, which saw practically all universities in South Africa being shut down by students for varying lengths of time in October and November. After the protests of 14 October, a number of universities that had not yet developed student movements outside of the existing politically-aligned student organisations, formed FMF movements (including UJ, University of the Western Cape (UWC), Cape Peninsula University of Technology (CPUT), and UKZN). In the cases of UCT, Rhodes, NMMU, UP and Wits, the existing student-led movements and formations outside of SRCs and politically-aligned student organisations existed alongside the emerging FMF movements.

The protests were initially largely directed at university managements that decide annually what the fee increases will be. University managements met with the Department of Higher Education and Training to try and quell the protests. On Tuesday 20 October 2015, the South African government, through the minister of Higher Education and Training, announced a capping of 2016 university fees across all institutions at 6%, in an attempt to calm the protests at campuses across the country. Students were unwilling to accept the compromise reached between university managements and the government. The student protests had elevated the issue of access to universities and government support of education into the national discourse, which resulted in many popular writings and analyses of the possibility and probability of an increase in government support for free, quality higher education.

Besides the historic disruption and shutting down of almost all universities towards the end of the academic year, just before final examinations were due to start, there were three significant events that took place exactly a week after the shut downs began. These three events indicated the expansion of the student protests to include a critique of, and action against, government's inadequate funding of higher education. On Wednesday 21 October students from universities across the Western Cape attempted to storm Parliament during the tabling of a budget report and insisted that the minister of Higher Education, Dr Blade Nzimande, come out to address them. Six students were arrested and later released. The minister came out and when he attempted to get the attention of the crowd by shouting the revolutionary call "Amandla!" (Power!), it was met with the response of "Ngawenu!" (With you!) instead of the usual "Ngawethu!" or "Awethu!" (With the people!). He did not manage to address the crowd who chanted #FeesMustFall and #BladeMustFall.

On the following day, 22 October, thousands of students in Johannesburg marched from UJ and Wits to Luthuli House, the headquarters of the ANC. There they delivered a memorandum to the ANC Secretary General Gwede Mantashe, but not before students made him come down to stand on the same level as them rather than address the crowd from the mobile stage that had been set up. There was a tense standoff when one of the student leaders insisted that Gwede Mantashe sit on the road with them, as thousands of students were seated. He refused and debated furiously with his aids and security personnel about whether he should leave. Eventually, one of the student leaders who was ANC-aligned redirected the energies and focused on the three memorandum points – the ANC government must:

1.   immediately release the funds to ensure a 0% fee increase for 2016 without universities imposing austerity measures.

2. urgently put forward a specific plan of action to realise free, quality higher education.
3. ensure it provides the resources to end outsourcing of workers immediately at institutions of higher learning.

The third day of action, Friday 23 October, saw thousands of university students, academics and workers march to the Union Buildings in Pretoria for an announcement by the ANC-led government. While the event was called for and organised by SASCO, an ANC-aligned student organisation, many people involved in the FMF protests marched. Many were determined not to allow the government to claim the freezing of fee increments for 2016 as their victory. The area of the Union Buildings looked and sounded like a war zone with police helicopters hovering overhead while students torched portable toilets and broke through a police barrier in an attempt to get closer to the main buildings. President Jacob Zuma announced via live television that there would be a 0% fee increase for 2016, which would be funded mostly by government, but no announcement was made directly to those gathered outside. The news filtered in via social media and news bulletins through those who had smart phones. The crowds on the lawns of the Union Buildings were not satisfied and wanted the president to come outside and address them directly. President Zuma did not appear and the police increased their attempts to disperse the crowd with stun grenades and later tear gas. Once the media and part of the crowd had left, the police swooped on the remaining people with stun grenades and tear gas and chased people with rubber bullets. Running battles between protesters and police continued after dark, eventually culminating with the arrest of seven TUT students, who later became known as the Sunnyside 7.

## Emerging solidarities

The joint actions by students, especially the marches to Parliament and the Union Buildings, meant that students who ordinarily would not struggle or protest together (like those from UCT, UWC, US and CPUT to Parliament, and Wits, UJ, UP and TUT to the Union Buildings), were united facing a common target, the state. Many historically-black universities like the TUT Soshanguve campus and UWC, whose students were largely black and poor, had been protesting about fee increases and financial exclusion, among other things, for a number of years. Private security and the police have been used to suppress these protests. This has meant that university student protesters at some institutions, particularly the historically-black institutions, have faced down batons, shields, stun grenades, rubber bullets and arrest for longer than the university protesters at historically-white institutions. 2015 was the year where this shifted. The protests at Parliament and the Union Buildings were the primary examples of students across institutions experiencing the same violent response from the police on behalf of government and university management.

The ANC-led government unofficially insisted that the student organisations aligned to it put a decisive end to the disruptive protest and accept the 0% fee increase decision as a victory. This led to a split in the FMF movement, with many students returning to class, and fewer students across all institutions continuing the struggle for free, decolonised education. Hostilities between ANC-aligned student organisations and alliances, and other student political parties like the Economic Freedom Fighters (EFF) and the Pan Africanist Student Movement (PASMA), increased, and the non-partisan student movements continued the struggle to decolonise South African universities. While the question of free higher education for the poor was the primary issue that government responded to, university managements were placed under enormous pressure by the student–worker alliance and its demand for an end to outsourcing. UCT was the first university to commit to insourcing,[3] on 28 October, followed on 1 November by Wits University's commitment, in principle, to insourcing. A number of universities have been forced to follow, with the major resistance against outsourcing coming from the #OutsourcingMustFall movement in early 2016, which was a joint protest among workers from UP, the University of South Africa (UNISA), TUT and Sefako Makgatho Health Sciences University (previously known as MEDUNSA), supported by students from these institutions.

Some universities began to use increasingly oppressive tactics against protesters. At UJ the university management's response was to securitise the campus but students and workers continued their protests in spite of the university and an outsourced company having four interdicts against protesting students and workers out at the same time. On 6 November the largest number of workers, students and academics, mostly from UJ but also from Wits, were arrested for being within 500 metres of the

UJ gate. The #Brixton163 spent the night in jail while large crowds gathered outside the police station to demand the release of their comrades. UWC and CPUT in Cape Town were two of the universities that saw the most violence, first between rival student organisations and later between private security companies aided by the police and students in the on-campus residences. UWC and CPUT were unable to hold any year-end examinations as a result.

Representatives from over twenty university FMF and earlier black-led student movements met for a national student movement workshop from 11 to 13 November 2015 in the south of Johannesburg and agreed on six long-term national demands for the broader student movement's consideration, that also applied to society as a whole:

1.  Free, quality, decolonised education from the cradle to the grave.
2.  An end to outsourcing and labour brokering.
3.  The decriminalisation of protest and protesters.
4.  An end to debt.
5.  A reformulation of governance structures to promote participatory rather than representative democracy.
6.  An end to all oppressive systems including racism, exploitation, sexism, homophobia, xenophobia, and ableism, amongst others.

While many people agreed that the student movements of 2015 were successful, there were also those who criticised the students. One of these critiques highlighted the extent of the violent disruptions and protests by students at various institutions. The broad student movement protests were largely peaceful but the tension between the ANC-aligned student organisations and SRCs continued to spread feelings of mistrust. The number of students at each institution who continued to struggle towards free, quality, decolonised education dropped for a range of reasons, not least because students were exhausted and had to prepare for and write exams in December and January. As the numbers of protesters dwindled and the end-of-year holiday period came around, students left for home to rest and spend time with their families. When students regrouped at the beginning of 2016, university managements, along with the government, were ready to stop any disruptive action from the student movements. This led to an increase of private security on campuses as well as interdicts taken out by university managements against students, in order for them to have police on standby. Besides costing universities millions of rands a month for this securitisation of campuses, it also created an atmosphere of fear and repression at many campuses. Student movements were forced to retreat from public spaces at the university as these were closely monitored by riot-police-style security. The 2016 registration period for university students largely ran smoothly as a result of these security measures, and the student movements have had to reassess their strategies to ensure that the goal of decolonised public African universities remains high on the agenda.

The first two months of 2016 saw university managements spend millions of rands to ensure that the status quo of university operations was not disrupted. Many universities were forced by student protest and action to delay the upfront or minimum fee payments for a few months, to limit the financial exclusions of students, and have been under extreme pressure to resolve the student housing crisis, all of which can be considered huge gains for the student movements. Universities became, in the space of a few weeks, places where student dissent was oppressed and closed down through interdicts and heavy-handed policing by private security guards and the South African Police Service. This resulted in student protesters using different forms of disruptive tactics, which in turn resulted in students receiving more violent dismissal, from beatings to arrests. The week of 15 February 2016 saw 51 students arrested at Walter Sisulu University (Mthatha, Eastern Cape), 8 students at UCT, 20 students at Wits, and 27 students at UP. University spaces have come to mirror what has been happening in poor communities over the last two decades, where people raising pertinent questions about inequality and oppression get criminalised.

Neville Alexander argues that:

> No government on earth can control the process of schooling completely.
> In fact, the schooling system is one of the Achilles heels of any ruling class.
> The beginnings of trouble in any modern society usually make themselves
> felt in the schools before they become evident in other institutions precisely
> because it is so difficult in a modern state to control this process.[4]

The student movement has been the single most significant movement to have woken government from its growing estrangement from the demands and needs of the people.

Let us hope that the responses that lie ahead are not driven by the impulse to suppress the important questions and demands that have been developed, but rather that the voices and questions of the youth of South Africa are taken seriously and engaged in a manner that will allow for all of us to contribute to building a better country and world.

## Endnotes

1    H. Bhorat, Is South Africa the most unequal society in the world? *Mail and Guardian*, 30 September 2015, http://mg.co.za/article/2015-09-30-is-south-africa-the-most-unequal-society-in-the-world.

2    Outsourcing is the cost-saving measure of an institution contracting the hiring of some staff to a cheaper third-party company that competes for the contract. In the case of universities, such companies provide security, cleaning, gardening and catering services on campuses. The workers doing these jobs are paid significantly less than if they were directly employed by the university and lose all the benefits that a regular university employee enjoys. These benefits include improved working conditions, job security, free tuition for children of workers to study at the universities their parents maintain, medical aid and paid leave for workers, among other things.

3    Insourcing refers to the students' campaign to pressure universities to reverse their policies of outsourcing workers and employ all staff directly.

4    N. Alexander, *Education and the Struggle for National Liberation in South Africa*, Johannesburg: Skotaville, 1990.

Leigh-Ann Naidoo is currently a PhD student in the School of Education at the University of the Witwatersrand. Her work is on the role of education in building social and political movements and her masters dissertation focused on the formation of the South African Students' Organisation (SASO) and the Black Consciousness movement and their relation to education. She is currently looking at questions related to the formation and role of black student intellectuals through a case study of the #RhodesMustFall (RMF) movement at the University of Cape Town. She is a co-convener of the Johannesburg Workshop in Theory and Criticism (www.jwtc.org.za) and was previously an Olympic beach volleyball player.

# SELECTED BIBLIOGRAPHY

Ansell, G. *Soweto Blues: Jazz, popular music and politics in South Africa*. London: Continuum, 2005.

Badat, S. *Black Student Politics: Higher education and apartheid from SASO to SANSCO, 1968–1990*. Pretoria: HSRC Press, 1999.

Baldwin, J. *The Fire Next Time*. New York: Dial Press, 1963.

Biko, S. *Steve Biko: I Write what I Like*. A. Stubbs (ed.). London: Heinemann, 1987.

Boesak, A. *Farewell to Innocence: A social-ethical study on Black Theology and Black Power*. Johannesburg: Ravan Press, 1976.

Brink, E., Malungane, G., Lebelo, S., Ntshangase, D. and Krige, S. *Recollected 25 Years Later – Soweto June 16: It all started with a dog*. Cape Town: Kwela Books, 2001.

Brookes, A. and Brickhill, J. *Whirlwind Before the Storm*. London: International Defence and Aid Fund for Southern Africa, 1980.

Coplan, DB. *In Township Tonight! Three centuries of black city music and theatre*. Johannesburg: Jacana, 2007.

Crenshaw, K. *On Intersectionality: The essential writings of Kimberlé Crenshaw*. New York: Perseus Distribution Services, 2012.

Davis, A. *Angela Davis: An autobiography*. New York: Bantam Books, 1975.

Delius, P. Mapping Histories of Rural Education: Where tradition and modernity clash, *Matlhasedi*, 1992, 11(1), July.

Diseko, N. The Origins and Development of the South African Students' Movement (SASM): 1968–1976, *Journal of Southern African Studies*, 1992, 18(1), 40-62.

Fanon, F. *The Wretched of the Earth*. New York: Grove Books, 2007.

Fatton, R. *Black Consciousness in South Africa: The dialectics of ideological resistance to white supremacy*. Albany: State University of New York Press, 1986.

Gerhart, GM. *Black Power in South Africa: The evolution of an ideology*. Berkeley: University of California Press, 1978.

Glaser, C. *Bo-Tsotsi: The youth gangs of Soweto, 1935–1976*. Oxford: James Currey, 2000.

Heffernan, A. Black Consciousness' Lost Leader: Abraham Tiro, the University of the North, and the seeds of South Africa's student movement in the 1970s, *Journal of Southern African Studies*, 2015, 41(1), 173-186.

Hirson, B. *Year of Fire, Year of Ash: The Soweto revolt – Roots of a revolution?* London: Zed Books, 1979.

Hlongwane, AK. The PAC in the Era of the 1976 Uprisings, *Journal of Pan African Studies*, 2009, 3(4).

Hlongwane, AK. The Historical Development of the Commemoration of the June 16, 1976 Soweto Students' Uprisings: A study of the re-representation, commemoration and collective memory, PhD Thesis, University of the Witwatersrand, 2015.

Hyslop, J. School Student Movements and State Education Policy: 1972–1987, in W. Cobbett and R. Cohen (eds.), *Popular Struggles in South Africa.* London: James Currey, 1988, 183-209.

Jeffery, A. *The Natal Story: Sixteen years of conflict.* Johannesburg: South African Institute of Race Relations, 1997.

Jeffery, A. *People's War: New light on the struggle for South Africa.* Cape Town: Jonathan Ball, 2009.

Johnson, S. The Soldiers of Luthuli: Youth in the politics of resistance in South Africa, in S. Johnson (ed.), *South Africa: No turning back.* Bloomington: Indiana University Press, 1988, 94-152.

Kane-Berman, J. *Soweto: Black revolt, white reaction.* Johannesburg: Ravan Press, 1978.

Kretschmar, L. *The Voice of Black Theology in South Africa.* Johannesburg: Ravan Press, 1986.

Lekgoathi, SP. Reconstructing the History of Educational Transformation in a Rural Transvaal Chiefdom: The radicalisation of teachers in Zebediela from the early 1950s to the early 1990s, Unpublished MA dissertation, University of the Witwatersrand, 1995.

Lodge, T. *Black Politics in South Africa since 1945.* Johannesburg: Ravan Press, 1983.

Lodge, T. and Nasson, B. (eds.). *All, Here and Now: Black politics in South Africa in the 1980s.* London: Hurst and Company, 1992.

Lorde, A. *Sister Outsider: Essays and speeches by Audre Lorde.* New York: Ten Speed Press, 1984.

Macqueen, I. Students, Apartheid and the Ecumenical Movement in South Africa, 1960–1975, *Journal of Southern African Studies*, 2013, 39(2), 447-463.

Magaziner, D. *The Law and the Prophets: Black Consciousness in South Africa, 1968–1977.* Athens: Ohio University Press, 2010.

Marks, M. *Young Warriors: Youth politics, identity and violence in South Africa.* Johannesburg: Wits University Press, 2001.

Mashabela, H. *A People on the Boil: Reflections on Soweto.* Johannesburg: Skotaville, 1987.

Mkhabela, S. *Open Earth and Black Roses: Remembering 16 June 1976.* Johannesburg: Skotaville, 2001.

Mokwena, SK. *A Blues for Tiro* (film), 2007.

Moloi, T. *Place of Thorns: Black political protest in Kroonstad since 1976.* Johannesburg: Wits University Press, 2015.

Moloi, T., Ndlovu, SM. and Nieftagodien, N. The Soweto Uprising (Parts 1–3), in South African Democracy Education Trust (SADET), *The Road to Democracy in South Africa: Volume 2, 1970–1980.* Pretoria: UNISA Press, 2006.

Morrow, S., Maaba, B. and Pulumani, L. *Education in Exile: SOMAFCO, the African National Congress school in Tanzania.* Pretoria: HSRC Press, 2004 [free download available at http://www.hsrcpress.ac.za/product.php?productid=1960].

Mzamane, MV. The Impact of Black Consciousness on Culture, in NB. Pityana et al., *Bounds of Possibility: The legacy of Steve Biko and Black Consciousness.* Cape Town: David Philip, 1991.

Ndlovu, SM. *The Soweto Uprising: Counter-memories of June 1976.* Johannesburg: Ravan Press, 1998.

Nieftagodien, N. *The Soweto Uprising: A Jacana pocket history.* Johannesburg: Jacana, 2013.

Nolan, A. *Jesus before Christianity.* London: Longman and Todd, 1977.

Nolutshungu, SC. *Changing South Africa: Political considerations.* Manchester: Manchester University Press, 1982.

Peterson, B. Culture, Resistance and Representation, in SADET, *The Road to Democracy in South Africa: Volume 2, 1970–1980.* Pretoria: UNISA Press, 2006.

Pityana, B., Ramphele, M., Mpumlwana, M. and Wilson, L. (eds.). *Bounds of Possibility: The legacy of Steve Biko and Black Consciousness.* Cape Town: David Philip, 1991.

Pohlandt-McCormick, H. I Saw a Nightmare: Doing violence to memory – The Soweto Uprising, June 16, 1976. PhD. Thesis, University of Minnesota-Twin Cities, 1999.

Prozesky, M. (ed.). *Christianity amidst Apartheid: Selected perspectives on the Church in South Africa.* London: Macmillan, 1990.

Republic of South Africa, *Report of the Commission of Inquiry into the Riots at Soweto and Elsewhere: Cillie Commission Report*, Pretoria: Government Printer, RP 55, Vol. 1, 1980.

Rueedi, F. The Politics of Difference and the Forging of a Political 'Community': Discourses and practices of the Charterist civic movement in the Vaal Triangle, South Africa, 1980–84, *Journal of Southern African Studies*, 2015, 41(6), 1181-1198

Seekings, J. *Heroes Or Villains? Youth politics in the 1980s.* Johannesburg: Ravan Press, 1993.

Van Kessel, I. *Beyond our Wildest Dreams: The United Democratic Front and the transformation of South Africa.* Charlottesville: University of Virginia Press, 2000.

Wa Thiong'o, N. *Decolonising the mind: The politics of language in African literature.* Nairobi: East African Educational Publishers, 1981.